Peter Darne

5 GUYS CHILLIN'

OBERON BOOKS
LONDON

WWW.OBERONBOOKS.COM

First published in 2016 by Oberon Books Ltd
521 Caledonian Road, London N7 9RH
Tel: +44 (0) 20 7607 3637 / Fax: +44 (0) 20 7607 3629
e-mail: info@oberonbooks.com
www.oberonbooks.com

A catalogue record for this book is available from the British
Library.

PB ISBN: 9781786829443
E ISBN: 9781786829436

Cover photo by Kasia Burke

FIVE GUYS CHILLIN'

'5 Guys Chillin' est au-delà d'une simple pièce de théâtre. On est plus dans un espace documentaire, vivant. Un documentaire qui se joue sous nos yeux. C'est une belle réussite dans un exercice pourtant assez difficile. Brute, cash, sans détour et très efficace. Bluffant.'

Franck Desbordes pour AgendaQ

'C'est quelque chose de brut, de dur, d'extrême et c'est couillu! Bref c'est à voir, ça donne à réfléchir, ça sensibilise sur un sujet bien plus grave et vaste qu'on ne le pense. Coup de coeur.'

Gaspard Granaud pour Pop and Films

'L'adaptation de cette pièce pousse le spectateur dans ses retranchements les plus intimes. Christophe Garro joue le jeu du faussement léger pour mieux nous acculer et nous questionner sur notre propre rapport à la sexualité… éveiller les consciences sur les dangers du chemsex. Dérangeant mais captivant… Le pari est réussi.'

Grégory Ardois-Remaud pour Qweek

Author's Note

I first met 'J' a few years ago. We lived close by. I had just moved to a different part of town, and he had not long moved to London for work. We became friends.

He was very open about the fact that he was discovering the 'chill' scene which, at that point, I had never heard of.

I was fascinated by the anarchic freedom that he seemed to live by, brave, sexually assured, confident in his looks and body, and an ability to get on with anyone. However, I was also aware of a buried sadness in him, dissatisfaction from previous failed relationships and a need for someone special to connect to. I also suspected that his nihilistic tendencies in part came from never having truly come to terms with his HIV status, or the way he contracted it. But whenever we met, J's stories were hilarious, and inspired me to create my play.

Gradually, over the course of the coming months, I saw J less often. If I visited him, other friends would turn up and make it evident that I should join in the drugs and chill they planned to have with him, or leave. He left the house less and less. I would arrange to go around, having first checked he was alone, to find him answering the door topless and high, with five or six strangers in the living room. If I questioned whether it was getting too much, he insisted on his right to do what he wants. He was just having a good time. And then he'd make me laugh with another outrageous story.

Here is where I find it difficult. Yes – in principal I agree to his right to do what he wants with his own body and to have a good time. And I also believe that some people can go through periods of their lives being drug users, not drug abusers. But when J lost his job, turned his house into a constant sex party, selling his car and borrowing tons of money to keep going, I no longer perceived it to be a great time. Or a choice. His ability to choose with free will had gone. But the J that chose to have a good time would not have believed that his relationship with drugs would turn into this downward spiral.

This play is dedicated to all the wonderful brave people who shared their stories with me.

The last time I visited him, after using his bathroom I came out to find him injecting Tina. He knows I don't like it. He looked at me and said 'I'm sorry Peter, but, it's just so fucking good'.

J came to see *5 Guys Chillin'* at the King's Head in its last run. He had been clean for forty-three days. I massively regret letting him come. The stress of being faced with that part of his life, in the company of his old chill mates, wasn't something he was ready for, and he relapsed.

I don't have any answers, and I'm certainly not making any judgments. Some people are in control. Some people think they are. Some people know they aren't. Some people don't know they aren't. There is a fine line between control and having fun, and being 'G'd' out in a stranger's flat.

I don't want to tell anyone not to do anything. But I don't want people to wander down roads blindly, and have the 'choice' that I respect, taken from them.

I hope this play shows some of the good times, some of the bad times, and encourages you think about what is right for you. It's your choice, no one else's. But let's all talk, look out for each other, and make our decisions with free will, from an informed place.

Peter Darney

Foreword by David Stuart

'ChemSex'.

'Chillout parties', 'chills'.

Gay orgies, drugs, HIV.

Terms guaranteed to ignite a war of passionate divided opinion amongst gay men, as well as to be fodder for media headlines, reminiscent of the anti-gay newspaper reports that were so common during the AIDS crisis circa 1985.

What's it all about? Peter Darney has been brave enough to explore it all in his new play, *5 Guys Chillin'*; and I do mean brave. I was honoured to be a regular attendee at the first few runs of this play, hosting some vibrant, sometimes heated post-show Q&A's with the audience. An audience left, frankly, disturbed by some of the issues they'd been confronted with during the performances. A small number walked out mid performance, overcome with emotions ranging from tears to anger. Those that remained afterward needed (seemingly urgently), to discuss and share the raw emotions they'd been left nursing. It was a responsibility and a privilege for me to be present for these Q&A's. And indeed brave of Peter Darney to address the very contentious and upsetting topic of ChemSex. Brave; but genius and loving of him to have done so through the prism of true stories. This is verbatim theatre.

Gay communities around the world are in the throes of a cultural shift; one that will require cool heads, kind hearts and possibly a little historical perspective to fully understand. ChemSex is a term coined by gay men on online sexual networking platforms, and simply means the use of drugs ('chems' – shorthand for 'chemicals') to improve (or enable) the experience of sex.

Nothing new there. Drugs and alcohol have played a part in the sexual pursuits of many populations throughout history. ChemSex however, has a unique definition.

Let's take, for example, heroin and crack cocaine. I don't think anyone will assume that these are recreational drugs. People don't use heroin to go out and have a laugh, to have a dance or a good time. Heroin and crack cocaine serve a very distinct purpose of numbing one's pain, of nursing historical trauma. In fact almost universally, associated with poverty, homelessness, crime and mental health. You might say, these drugs are preferred for their dissociative qualities. Not social drugs. The high is quite an isolating, comforting one.

Gay men have always favoured 'party drugs' over heroin and crack cocaine. Throughout the 1980s, 90s and early 2000s, gay men were using ecstasy, MDMA, cocaine – in quite large numbers. Some UK research demonstrated that gay men's drug use is seven times higher than their heterosexual counterparts. Why these drugs? People use different drugs for different purposes. Many gay men grow up as the only gay in the family. Sometimes, the only gay in the school. The only gay in the village. Quite an isolating experience. They're unlikely then, to choose a drug that isolates them further. They'd be more likely to choose a drug that facilitates connection, community even. Drugs that improve confidence, bring people together, perhaps on a dance-floor with other like-minded people also seeking connection, community. Ecstasy, MDMA, cocaine have served gay people and communities well in this regard, particularly through some lonely coming-out experiences or through a harrowing AIDS epidemic.

And though a lot of this drug use was about dancing and clubbing, let's not assume for a moment, that there wasn't a lot of sex occurring on these drugs. A hell of a lot of sex was occurring on these drugs. Fortunately though, ecstasy, MDMA and powdered cocaine are remarkably less dangerous than heroin and crack cocaine. In fact, throughout the 1980s, 90s and early 2000s, despite the common use of party drugs, we did not see gay men rushing to Accident and Emergency departments with overdoses from these drugs. We did not see gay men suffering dangerous withdrawal symptoms, or requiring urgent detoxes. We didn't see large numbers of gay men accessing drug support services with injecting drug use problems, or seeking help with addictions. And we did not see remarkable rises in HIV or other sexually-transmitted infections as a result of this recreational drug use.

But then something happened. A few things in fact.

Almost overnight, the way gay men sought sex, connection and community changed, with the adoption of new technologies. Geosexual networking Apps and websites (such as Gaydar, Grindr et al) introduced us to faster ways of finding sex, introduced us to new ways of communication. A good thing for the most part. The sometimes dangerous culture of seeking sex and love through 'cottaging' in public toilets or parks ended almost overnight, in favour of online dating and sex-seeking. In a way, these Apps de-shamed the historically illegal gay sex, bringing it proudly into the 21st century and onto our smartphones.

A downside? These Apps didn't come with any instruction booklet. Bonds of pre-hooking-up intimacy that had been formed in bars, perhaps over a drink or a first date, were now being replaced with clumsy, abbreviated attempts to communicate our sexual and emotional needs via an online platform, with a limited number of characters in a 'profile', and accompanied by an avatar that advertised our sexiness in competition with countless others. That's quite a skill-set for a population of people who are (arguably) sexually and emotionally vulnerable, having endured decades of cultural homophobia, illegality and a traumatic and stigmatising HIV epidemic. Amid this clumsiness, grew new stigmas; sexual rejections, poorly-informed, based on race, effeminate qualities or body fitness fascism became a new ways of shaming or isolating sections of our community. HIV stigma found a new public platform to be aired. Again; no instruction booklet to guide us through this minefield of intimacy-seeking.

But that's not all; at the same time that we were adjusting to this sexual/technological revolution, three new drugs landed, almost overnight, in the laps of gay communities. These drugs were crystal methamphetamine, mephedrone and GHB/GBL. These drugs became more easily available to larger numbers of gay men with the advent of smartphone Apps; one did not require a dealer or a real-life social network to procure drugs; one only had to log in and find someone within GPS range willing to share chems. Furthermore, these three drugs were significantly more dangerous than the party drugs we'd been accustomed to. Capable of delivering an incredibly more potent, sexually-disinhibiting 'high', these drugs have more addictive potential, and are associated with greater risk and harms than the comparatively innocent ecstasy, MDMA and powdered cocaine favoured by our forebears.

Since 2005, we have seen increasing numbers of gay men rushed to Accident and Emergency departments with overdoses, or withdrawal symptoms requiring urgent medical detoxes. We are seeing higher numbers of drug facilitated sexual assaults. More gay Londoners are injecting drugs than ever before in recorded history (according to Public Health England), and greater numbers of gay men are seeking support from drug services. The greatest public health concern however, is reflected in the rises in HIV and other sexually transmitted infections that accompanied the uptake of these drugs by gay communities. The UK's first targeted NHS ChemSex support service was opened in 2010 at 56 Dean Street in London's Soho. Over 3,000 gay men using chems access 56 Dean Street each month, and similar presentations are being observed in the Americas, Australia, Asia and Europe. In 2012, 90% of the HIV positive men accessing London's Antidote drug and alcohol support services attributed their HIV diagnoses to the use of chems.

ChemSex invites further debate, about the role sex plays in the lives of gay men in 2016. Some argue we are too highly sexualised as culture, angering those who, for decades, have fought the case for gay sexual liberation, without being forced into 'hetero-normative' boxes. Debates are waged over whether saunas are appropriate parts of gay culture while an HIV epidemic is hampered by promiscuity and chem-use. Others believe historical and cultural homophobia have contributed to an unconscious shame around gay sex that may encourage gay men to seek the disinhibition of chems for sex. This angers other sections of our communities, who defiantly claim to be shame-free. More still, debate that thirty years of AIDS and HIV have inextricably linked gay sex with risk and danger, encouraging gay men to seek escapism from this risk in a drug high. Or to have a dismissive attitude to risk and danger, ignoring the harms associated with chems. These debates also fuel community debate about PrEP, a new HIV prevention drug that can prevent HIV transmission without the use of condoms.

More than simply a 'drug problem', ChemSex is a culturally unique phenomenon. And it is divisive, so divisive. Gay sex, promiscuity, disease, drug use, differing addiction definitions… it is a melting pot for moral judgment, fear and stigma. From a public health perspective, it is no more than a syndemic of behaviours affecting a particularly vulnerable population, and one which requires an effective public health response. But from a community perspective … we have a problem.

This is where the role of theatre is invaluable. Theatre has a proud tradition of providing the forum in which challenging social issues can be explored. Bringing ChemSex to the stage as Peter Darney has with *Five Guys Chillin'*, not only raises awareness of this difficult cultural phenomenon, but provides a safe space for the issues to be presented, explored, humanised; extricated from the scandal-mongering headlines that alarm and stigmatise the issue.

That's not to say it's an easy ride; this script does not shy away from the harsh realities of ChemSex. Nor does it shy away from the controversy. One act into this play, and you know that this is not the Disney interpretation of ChemSex. Two acts in, and you know that Peter is not trying to win friends or praise from this story. Nor is he prepared to hide behind fiction; every word in this play is verbatim from the mouths of babes with real experiences of ChemSex, interviewed for the purpose of an accurate script.

I'd argue that Peter Darney's purpose was, simply, truth; it's among the most heartfelt of any scripts I've seen brought to life. In the 1980's, an AIDS awareness campaign stated simply, that 'Silence = Death'; ChemSex is imbued with so many unpleasant truths, it can be tempting to avoid it. It can be so tempting to just blame others, some irresponsible 'others' who are letting the side down, embarrassing the gay community, undoing the freedoms we have achieved over the last forty years.

But it is a problem for all of us, whether we use chems or not. Just as HIV is a problem for all of us whether we have it or not. This is a community issue, one that will require compassion, unity, and the setting aside of our judgments and unkindness. Silence is not an option as we all, as a community, strive to address this embarrassing and morally challenging problem. Theatre and the arts may well be the safest and most perfect forum to raise and explore the controversy of ChemSex; and I thank Peter Darney for this brave and extraordinary production.

David Stuart is the Substance Use Lead at 56 Dean Street addressing the sexualised drug use by gay men (the practice commonly referred to as 'ChemSex'). He has been involved in the development of London's pioneering services Antidote, Club Drug Clinic and CODE clinic, and has been instrumental in placing ChemSex issues firmly on international Public Health agendas. He has been consulted by the governments and public health bodies of many countries across Europe, Australia and USA, including the World Health Organisation/UNAIDS. He is a researcher, writer and lecturer on the issues of sexual wellbeing, substance use and HIV.

David's work is the subject of the feature documentary from ViceUK, 'ChemSex'.

David is also the curator of the Dean Street Wellbeing programme, a series of community engagement events that resource art and theatre, designed to mobilise and engage populations in action and dialogue on topical and challenging social issues that impact sexual health and wellbeing.

Characters

J: The action takes place in his flat. J is friends with M, but has never met the others before tonight. He is a funny, kind, vulnerable and witty raconteur. His drug taking has a firm grip on his life and he often hosts chillouts that last for days. In his early thirties he was a designer before his addiction to the scene meant that he was no longer able to work.

M: He is a tall, good-looking American who has lived in London for some years. Slightly aloof, he is cynical of the scene, but he keeps returning to it. He is friends with J, but has not met any of the others before tonight. He works in film PR, is able to maintain his job and is reasonably well-off.

B: Partner of R, he is meeting the others for the first time this evening. More of a 'bear/Recon' type. Forties. Tattooed, in shape. Very self-assured, confident. B has an aggressive edge, and a touch of belligerence. He is into a more S&M or hard-core scene. He works as a casting director in Porn.

R: Partner of B. Slightly younger, sweet lovely guy – alternative-looking in real life. Very chatty, open and honest, and gets along with anyone. He works in a sex shop, although his drug-taking has meant that he has collapsed at work several times. His job is in now the balance.

PJ: Pakistani Male, late twenties/early thirties. Not such a frequent partygoer, and doesn't take so many drugs. He is married, his wife is pregnant with their second child. He has a light accent, having been raised mostly in London. In his main life, he has a reasonably ordinary heterosexual middle-class life. Chill parties are his only real outlet for his true sexuality, making him very highly sexed once he gives into his urges.

5 Guys Chillin' was first performed at Otherplace Brighton on 22–25 May 2015 and transferred to the King's Head London from the 1 October – 28 November 2015

Director: Peter Darney

Movement: Chris Cuming

Lighting Designer: Sherry Coenen

Sound Designer: Jo Walker

Associate Director: Julie Addy

Brighton Assistant Director: Linda Miller

Edinburgh Assistant Director: Samson Hawkins

Cast

J: Damien Hughes	(later Matthew Bunn)
M: Tom Holloway	(later Tom Kay)
R: Elliot Hadley	
B: Michael Matovski	
PJ: Shri Patel	(later Amrou Al-Kadhi)

It was revived from the 5-27 February at the King's Head Theatre, and transferred to the Dublin International Gay Theatre Festival and to the Warren Theatre at Brighton Fringe with the cast as follows:

J: Gareth Kennerley

M: Haydn Whiteside

R: Elliot Hadley

B: Michael Matovski

PJ: Cael King

Edinburgh Festival, C Too, 4–29 August 2016

J: Matthew Bunn

M: Cesare Scarpone

R: Elliot Hadley

B: Michael Matovski

PJ: Adi Chugh

A massive thank you to: David Stuart, Patrick Cash, 56 Dean St, Spencer Watts, Kasia Burke Photography, James Hogan, Shane Kinghorn, Nicola Hayden and the Otherplace team, Adam Spreadbury-Maher and The King's Head team, Lucy Darney, Desmond Darney, David Roberts-Lock, The Terrence Higgins Trust, Positive East, Freedoms Shop, Linda Miller, Oscar Blustin, Brian Merriman, Prof Brett Kahr, Jane Dodd, The Blewbury Players, Radio Reverb, Richard Holliday, ALRA, Sarah Double, Bristol Old Vic, Michelle Paul, Ricky McFadden, Clonezone, Giles Ramsay, Alex Enmarch, Edgar Trujillo Gonzalez.

The action takes place in the living room of a flat. It could be anywhere, any style. There could be a mattress in the middle of the room. There is a laptop or TV and Sound System. There are Porn DVD cases.

All the characters have been talking on mobile phone apps prior to the party, and have arrived through meeting on Grindr, Scruff etc.

When working on the play, rehearsals should be focused on finding the subtext and story of the party. Who agrees/ disagrees/related to the last story told? How have the drugs impacted? Who wants who? If looked for, there is always some trigger in what the last person said that the next person is picking up on to trigger what they are saying. The main aim is find the story of the party you're creating, through relationships, cause and effect, and subtext.

Preset. All the bellow is set to music, and is choreographed action. As the audience enters J is on stage watching The X Factor on a laptop, also watching his phone for messages, restless. After some hesitation he goes off, then comes on again with drugs including Mephedrone. He cuts and snorts two lines of the drug.

He looks at Grindr on his phone, sends a message, keeps checking for a response.

Grindr bleeps.

M arrives, takes his coat off, settles, snorts a line. They both watch The X Factor.

On front of house clearance M changes The X Factor to a club tune he loves.

Grindr bleeps.

M is slightly annoyed. J shows him R and B's pics on his phone and tells him they have arrived. M grudgingly accepts.

R and B arrive. They all greet.

J goes off – R turns up the music.

J brings chillout things (EG; sheets/towels/shorts/lube and poppers).

After a pause – agreement between the four.

They dress the space for a chillout, maybe covering the sofa, or putting out throws.

They undress and put on chillout things (shorts/singlets/jocks/harness etc.)

When they are dressed Grindr bleeps.

They rush to the phone. J shows the group PJ's pic. They agree. He arrives.

They greet – he is awkward.

J offers PJ a line – he declines.

J *(Turns down the music and asks PJ:)* So go on, tell me, is this your first chill? *(General adlibs of 'Aww' and 'Bless'.)*

R: *(Before* PJ *can answer.)* I think the first sex party I ever went to, I suppose sex party wasn't what it was called then, but I went to a 'group sex session' when I was sixteen or seventeen?

J: *We* called it a *group session* too. It sounds a bit *primitive,* doesn't it? Me and my ex used to do them a bit. Host them. In Glasgow. *(Aimed at* M.*)* Despite people's belief that chillouts haven't reached other parts of the country – it isn't true!

PJ: No – I was about sixteen, and I didn't think I really realised it was a chillout. I was meant to be meeting this guy, and he had some other people there. And I was just kind of curious, and promiscuous, so I just went with it.

M: *(Wanting to join in.)* Somebody I was dating, he lived with, a couple who had chillouts *every* Saturday. And that's how I sort of … Got introduced to them. It was slightly, sort of surprising? Because of the drugs that people take. This was like a *first date!!*

R: We kind of just all sat around, tossed each other off, then sucked each other off, then fucked each other. And that was *(Through laughter.)* kind of how it was!

PJ: Mine wasn't a chillout in the sense you have them now, where it's very drug-fueled. They were playing classical music! *(Pointing at B.)* I just remember this really old guy lounging on a big sofa, in quite a nice apartment, and he had a massive dick, which I spent a lot of time on! *(Laughs.)* That was it really – just a bit of an orgy on a Sunday afternoon.

B: OK – I was a bit of a late starter when it comes to sex parties. I'd been in monogamous long-term relationships up until my early thirties … And then when I came out of an eight-year relationship, I found myself … with urges to go and explore what else was out there – see what I could find. So I went to a sex club in Manchester … Met up with a couple of guys I'd spoke to on bare back real time … And they said 'Oh we're going back to somewhere after this … Do you wanna to come with us.' And so I did.

R: I was at a rave in Glasgow, with some straight friends, and everyone was chattin' about it, and I thought I'll just turn up and see what it's like … it was a mixed party … bisexual – because at the time I was still playing with girls *(J and M repulsed, making PJ more awkward.)* … um … it was *(Through laughter.)* very different to the type of parties we do now!! … Favorite bit being a guy would cum in a fanny, and then

I would, like, lick it out and … Spit it in someone's face, or summat. *(Laughs.)* As you do!

B: I remember the car journey back – It was six of us in a *Ford Fiesta* … all off our tits on Ketamine, including the driver. Funny … When I got back to the party it was just so … relaxed … and straight forward – if you wanted to play with someone you go and play with them. If you wanted to sit and chill, you'd sit and chill. I remember thinking this is the kind of party that I wanna do … The kind of fun that I suit.

PJ: I had sex with four guys. *(Teasing reactions.)* I don't think I was very good at it, at the time. *(Laughs.)* I think I was just like really scatty. I wasn't very sure of myself. I didn't have sex because I wanted to have sex – coz I fancied a guy. It was all pent up – frustration, anxiety, and all that stuff that needed to come out? And it was more kind of – how far can I go? I guess to mirror what was going on in my own mind, coz I was quite confused about a lot of things?

Awkward pause.

J: *(Trying to divert PJ from his over-sharing.)* Talking of *confusing*, there was a guy sat there last night injecting his penis with Caverject.

M: What's that?

J: It's Viagra in injection form.

M: OMG – wow! I find needles very difficult to cope with!

J: In those sorts of areas, yeh! He was paranoid that he wouldn't get hard! … It's all a bit sad really. It's almost like if you don't have a hard on you're not … valid in a chillout? *(He goes for PJ's cock.)*

PJ: *(Jumping up.)* I'm a Pakistani male from a very traditional family, it's never gonna be accepted, you know? There's a part of me that – I will never like myself. That drove me to do things that I didn't particularly like doing. I can't say I didn't like all of it. But I would just do everything *(Laughs – others join in to try and pull him back to being positive.)* to see how much I could tolerate? And that was fun actually, because I can tolerate a lot, and I'm quite strong. *(Others react – 'shotgun' etc.)* So yeh, I knocked on this door – I was quite nervous – but I was really, really horny.

B: *(Coming on to PJ.)* Going to someone's house for the first time is always a bit of a strange experience – and when there's sex involved as well…

PJ: I got fucked by a few people. And then afterwards, I felt a little bit … grossed out, to be honest, and I remember I would always feel a little bit … embarrassed, and disgusted at myself. But that was also the bit that I liked. I wanted it to match how I felt inside. A little bit disgusted at myself. A little bit ashamed.

Pause. Everyone is awkward at this disclosure. B saves the day.

B: I nearly got fisted for the first time! I didn't, coz the guy's hands were like hammers!

M: At your first chill? How does *that* come about? What conversation happens?

B: So someone could be playing with your ass … And then at some point … Maybe they could say 'are you into fisting?'

23

... or it could be something that just evolves from ass-play. Fisting's a bit of a marmite sex act, you either love it or you hate it. And y' know some people they just don't get it ... It's sticking your hand in someone's ass – wow, what do I, as a top, get out of that – whereas ... If you're really into it, it ... It's something! It's the closest I've come to a spiritual experience. Because you're so deeply connected with the other person, so ... In tune with everything that's going on – inside and out of that person ... It goes beyond fucking ... Fisting is much more ... sensual. Because when you've got so much of you inside someone else, the tiniest movement is amplified ... like ten times.

B hands M lube – through the next M makes out he is getting ready to fist B, to B's delight.

M: I've been to chillouts where I've seen guys twenty-one, twenty-two ... getting double fucked ... fisted. Fist-fucking was something I never even fathomed happening at that age, you know? And you know these twenty-one-year-old bottoms, hungry, just wanna get bigger cocks, bigger cocks, bigger cocks and get fucked all weekend, and I'm just like ... *(Slaps B's ass and laughs – he has been teasing him – massive group reaction.)* Wow!! You know, seriously? You're gonna have to be wearing *tampons* when you're older to stop yourself from shitting. Which happens.

B: *(M helps B up, be digs at M.)* Something I've noticed, the difference between North an' South, in Manchester, people have a laugh – you know? You're getting ready for a fuck party, and people are joking about – being friendly. In London? It's all clinical – they're not interested in who you are as a person.

M hugs B and apologises.

R: I think in London it's more about the drug, rather than the party? The party part in London's missing? Down here – you don't go to a sex party, you go to a chill out to do drugs and have sex … But then you do drugs and then you can't have sex! *(Everyone agrees.)* Everyone's sitting around on their phones … Grinding … Scruffing … They don't interact with each other to have sex … And we turn up, sometimes as the entertainment, to try and get the sex to happen?

M: Entertainment?

B: Well I'm a bit of an instigator!

R: As am I!

B: If I'm in a room full of people who aren't engaging with each other – throw me in the middle of it and I'll try and get people interacting and having sex.

M: *(To PJ – who is still fully dressed, to get him to change.)* The worst thing is, when you arrive? In this sort of group situation? … and use just sort of wanna … You got your clothes on!!!! *(R takes PJ to change/undress.)* You just wanna maybe put some shorts on – chillout! … Shorts is a big thing! Easy access! They look hot. You're not going to go to a chillout to put on a pair of long johns are you? I find it quite amusing 'D'you wanna pair of shorts ?'… D'you wanna shot of G? D'you wanna line of Meph?' We should have usherettes walking round with trays!

PJ is in shorts – group appreciation.

R: *(Going to J.)* There's always a host to the party. And like for me – *(Flirting.)* I make an effort to play with the host … Whether they're to my taste or not! So once you start having sex with someone or doing a sexual act – that kind of – flicks everyone else – wakes them up to think – actually, *(Chasing PJ playfully.)* we're here for sex – not to just sit around and chat – d'y' know what I mean?

B, R and J get sexual through this.

B: A sex party to me it's where guys are going to fuck, and it becomes very Caligula orgy-esque

R: Sodom and Gomorrah – let's all just fuck each other – *(They realise the others aren't ready for sex yet and that they are freaking PJ out and making M uncomfortable.)*

B: Whereas a chill is more about guys chilling out, taking some drugs, maybe looking to see if there's any other guys around – not necessarily having sex –

R: It's about relaxation

B: It's about relaxation and hanging out.

M: You chat to people, see what the vibes like, you know – you walk in, they walk in … and sometimes you are just there for sex, but you still need to have that little moment of … okay. This is a good environment. I'm gonna stay here …

J: But a chill can turn into a sex party.

J & R: Yeh!!!

R: Or a sex party can turn into a chill … Coz if you've been playing, for six, seven hours, there is a point when you say – we need to take a break! That's when the chill bit starts to happen.

J: But obviously the mood of a party can change, you know? If two people decide to start a bit of fun in the corner? I don't think people would ever say 'This is purely a chill out, People will *not* be having sex.'

M: I can't remember the last time I went out and met somebody, like, at a bar? Drinking? And had sex with them. Now it's so instant …'Hung'… *(With sarcasm.)* 'Okay hi how are you!' *(Laughs.)* I hate that and I always reply – 'No, I'm tiny – why? Are you loose and sloppy!' And fifty per cent of the time they'll respond yes! … I'm like 'ewww – god – Jeeesus Christ! That's horrible!' And I've had people respond me, like send a message saying 'I want you to spunk up my sloppy poz hole' and I'm just like *(Pretends to puke.)* – think I've got dishes to do.

J: I think I may have that on my laptop!

B: We try and let people choose whatever porn they want … Coz porn can be a bit … prescriptive?

R: For me it doesn't really do much. I find it a little bit clinical, and boring? I find somebody actually having sex more, arousing – so I tend to put on videos of *us* playing with other people coz that actually arouses me more. Or I'm – I'm totally addicted to Tumblr at the moment…

They all go to the computer to look.

…people who – toss themselves off, or fuck someone and post it on Tumblr –
I like /that more than

B: /I think if something's real – not scripted … It's more horny to watch … coz you know that the guys that are doing it are actually enjoying themselves.

R: I'll sit there and I'll literally go – ergh – they missed a total really good camera angle, or … Light's shining in completely the wrong place, or that's not even real cum, or – the guys actually don't like each other? You can see they're like, blank faced, they've obviously taken something to get their cocks so hard to play with each other. But I'm a very big voyeur. I get off on watching that more than actually engaging myself. I get off on watching him get fucked a lot.

B: I mean this is it – you don't need to sit watching porn when you've got John and Tom over there and Ban and Jerry over there fucking the shit out of each other.

R: Mmm – I just sit and have a wank *(Laughing.)* while other people are fucking around – stick a dildo in you – you're like 'here you go – use that as well – haha – stick that in – stick that up your arse' – then stick a cock in as well – fold it in half and put that in as well!!!

B: Well – it becomes the ultimate interactive porn, doesn't it?

R: Yeh! On a, on a DVD you can't suddenly go – 'Oooh, yeh, let me shove my cock in there as well'… whereas, if there's a couple of guys and you're like, 'do you fancy some DP?' And you go and join in – stick your finger in – or you stick your hand up, and wank someone off inside someone else …

B shows the group a graphic picture on his phone, they all recoil. M changes the subject.

M: Ew my God!

R: To start with, for me – it probably didn't happen that often coz I was always in relationships. *(Surprised reactions from the group.)* I always tended to choose partners who were quite vanilla. And then I got myself into a long-term monogamous relationship. I think – towards the end of that I – *We* opened – So we'd go to the pub, choose who we wanted. Then take them home and fuck the shit out of them. Drugs was never involved, coz like the partner I was with at the time was massively against drugs. I'd been a massive drug addict before I was with him, so not doing drugs was, like, really good for me! And we broke up, and then I-I-I ended up with this lovely one

B: *(Annoyed.)* With this lovely one, thanks.

R: No, we're like, really similar … in too many ways – coz we encourage each other. I never used to be a jealous person, but I find myself jealous every now and again –

B: *(More annoyed.)* What?

R: *(Trying to get out of the awkwardness.)* Not jealous of you being with other people – just jealous that I'm not there to be involved – but … meh!!! We have more parties now than I've ever had in my life. But only because we both enjoy it. Situation is – like last weekend, we went to the pub, then the sauna, we brought a couple of guys back with us – played with them – then invited another couple of guys over – then another couple of guys came over. Then I went to work – didn't I? – in between! I went to work for/a few hours

B: Left me /at home

R: /and then left you at home with them – went to work, came back, carried on, then went back to work later, came back and carried on! But that's how we play! Not all the time. But it is *(Laughing.)* the majority at the moment!!

PJ: So you throw parties – and go to them together and separately?

R: Yeh?

B: Yeh

R: Yes … we used to go separately, but mur – mostly we go together now, don't we? … erm … yeh …

B: Yeh.

R: Yeh.

M: You know that some people do it and seem to have a great time, they are usually the very attractive, great bodies, good-looking, big cocks type of guys … can walk into any room and everybody wants them … But if you're not like that, you do it, you risk … being rejected whilst high, which can be even worse. Coz you – you just spiral out – you know, you just, do more drugs to … numb that pain and … it just doesn't work!

B: But your confidence also becomes more attractive to other people. So then you're invited to more parties – it reaches a point where you have to say 'no' but …

R & B: *(Together.)* We will party!

B: Every other weekend I go to Wales to see my children, which gives me a break from the sex … And gives him a break … Because you can imagine if I didn't have that … We'd be partying more!!

B&R: Yeh *(They laugh.)*

B: If we go on holiday, I like to go somewhere where I know that there's gonna be sex clubs … sex bars … a good party scene …

R: Don't really do family holidays, do we!

B: No … Well if we do it's only coz we're looking for daddies to fuck!

R: Yeh … Sex does kind of take over your life … It can if you let it …but/

B:/Sex takes over your life, completely … but we have our third who rains us in. When he's here we play a lot less coz he's a lot more shy than we are, he's like – when we're like *(Together.)* yeh! *He's* like *(Together.)* 'No'!

M: Rewind – a third?

R: Yeh, there's three of us in our relationship … We have like a polymorphic triad relationship.

B: Polyamorous!

R: Polyamorous, yeh!

B: Polymorphic? Tut!

R: Shut up! So there's three of us – me and him, and, the other. So, when he's here, we play less. Probably because there's no need, there's three of us, so you've already got group sex.

M: Do you all sleep in the same bed?

R: Yeh … we have a very WIDE bed *(Laugh.)* It works really – it works alright, doesn't it?

B: Yeh.

R: Can get stressful.

M: Is your relationship the central part of this polyamorous relationship?

R: *(Together.)* Yes, it's …

B: *(Together.)* Not really, no.

R: *(Awkwardly backtracking.)* No, the relationship's kind of secondary … to our lifestyle … Parsay (sic) isn't it.

> *Things are a little awkward as the others realise that R is more into B than B is into R.*

J: What drugs do you take?

R: My favorite is MDMA … Just because it makes you kind of float around a little bit? It's kinda like whooooo I'm really happy*! (J gives R some MDMA – they dab, M comes over and does a bump. J starts prepping the G-shots.)* I'm not, I'm not a big lover of … drugs that make you lose yourself – I just – I like drugs that make you happy. It's like when I was younger I used to take E … I would do Speed, Coke – but now my favorite's MDMA. I've done Tina, I do Mephedrone – that's what we do the most really isn't it? – not that blue Meph – he went blind!! 'G' … doesn't work for me I get actually quite ill. Usually about ten – fifteen minutes later I'm either puking or shitting myself … *(Laughing.)* So I try to stick away from it, but then you know you're like, everyone's like 'G time' you're like – 'Oh go on then!', and then you're like 'Ooh fuck – why did I do that?!' –

B: Why do you do that?

PJ: What is G?

J: G is a liquid drug. I think it's GHB? Administered in controlled small doses … can give you quite a buzz. Which seems to work very well with sex, I find! *(PJ, J and B do their G-shot and wince.) (To M.)* How do you find it?

M: I've never done it.

J: *(Shocked.)* Why not?

M: Because I saw four people successively G-out last time I was here!

J: Really? Was I one of them?

M: Yeh!

J: And am I alive now?

M: Yeh!

J: Am I healthy?

M: Hmmmm

J: Relatively! *(Laughs.)*

M: What about the other three?

J: Yeh, they're still alive. I think!

M: Do you know who they are?

J: No.

M: Then how do you know they're alive?

J: Because surely someone would have mentioned it in the feedback forms!

Group laughter. PJ is scared – adlibbed reassurance.

R: But it counterbalances the Mephedrone which I always used to snort. I've only really been slamming for say three? Four? Four months. I wanted to know why is everyone doing it now – Mer-Ma-Mer-Ma-Mer – what's so good about it? And I slammed Tina ... And was like ew ... What's that ... But then I slammed Mephedrone and that was really exhilarating ... And it kind of reminded me of something I used to get from Speed and it's like *(Sucks in.)* and you kinda get the ooh *(Sucks in.)* hello I'm like really happy like *(Sings.)* la-la-ah alright then ...

J: I find Mephedrone relaxing – it's just like having a bottle of wine really ... It just gives you a little bit of a ... although it's an upper ... chills you out I suppose ... Makes you feel slightly less concerned about things, yeh? Unless you have too much of it, for a long period of time, coz then you do start getting a bit over-thinky.

R: I'm very in in controls of drugs ... I have let them take control of me before – I'm very perceptive and aware of who's taking what and what time they're taking it. And it's usually after I've left, something happens, and I come back and ...

B Kisses R aggressively to shut him up. A very awkward moment. PJ goes to M and J. J gets out the Tina pipe to save the mood.

B: Smoking Tina gives you ulcers in your mouth. If you slam it, it all goes in you ... so you're not wasting any.

J looks tempted. M shakes his head. J declines.

M: That's just taking it far too far too far, yeh!

B: You can snort it.

R: But it /burns

B: /It is harsh to snort. If I slam Tina I'll slam between a quarter to a half a gram in one go – and that will see me through for a day.

R: But then sometimes, other guys bring drugs with them – that's when you get into a situation where you're like let's have another slam, let's have another slam!

B: And what starts off at just maybe one or two /slams

R: /Turns into about seventeen! Because obviously your drugs might run out but … when you're the host of a party – 'Here you go – that's a little bit for the host!'

J: You hope what goes around comes around! And that's been proven, given that I was very generous with my drugs and times are hard now … and I've met a drug dealer that keeps me going in return for sexual favours!

R: *(To J.)* On my arm here I had a boil from … I don't even know what from really … obviously from slamming. *(Laughs.)* So I do myself, and if I can't do myself I will let him do it, but only because I trust him. A lot of people get off on the act of watching a slam.

B: Yeh. There's a phenomena now of people videoing a slam happening and posting it on the internet!

R: Yeh – so if somebody says to me 'can I slam you' I'd go, I'd be like – 'Er… Yeh – but I'll put the needle in, and I'll prepare it' and all they then have to do is push the the the the *(Laughing.)* the bit down *(Both laugh hard.)* and then it's done … But otherwise I was always a snorter … I still enjoy snorting drugs.

B: I don't, I really don't like snorting drugs.

M: Injecting yourself with drugs is just that borderline addiction to heroin – crack den type scenario – it's not sexy. You know people after they slam – half the time they look like they've got special needs! It's not sexy. It's not a turn on.

J snogs and blowbacks M to calm him down.

J: I don't have a job, so I will get high of an evening or whatever – I'll probably not sleep – or I'll pass out about five a.m., wake up at about eleven a.m. having missed some form of job seeking appointment or something like that. And there'll be a couple of lines left over. And then I'll think – 'Oh fuck it, I'll just clear the plate'. Well you don't, coz you just go and get another bag afterwards. And then the process starts again – y'know what I mean? But for me that's – I wouldn't say – it's not – I don't think – an addiction? *(Group agrees it isn't.)* It's just because it's there.

R: Why do us gays take so many drugs?

M: Wait wait wait, lots of communities take lots of drugs. There is a banker community, a lawyer community that do a lot of Coke, or other stuff. I know doctors and professors in medicine who are functioning heroin addicts. Lots of people do it. I think for us, sex is much more of a pastime than it is for anyone else. That very visceral experience ... and drugs enhance that.

Movement transition: R puts music on – 'tune' they dance – rush – high – time passes – they collapse enjoying the rush/high. Maybe take some clothes off. B and J collapse snogging/playing on the sofa. J turns the music down to take us back to real time. M and PJ are the last ones standing, PJ directs the following to him, and to R.

PJ: I've always been gay – I went to *gay* clubs when I was fourteen with my sisters and their gay mates. In Punjabi culture you kind of have this pressure on you to carry the family name and inherit the land. And you're also responsible for taking care of the parents. So I never kind of thought that I *wouldn't* get married, but at the same time it just didn't seem to *fit* with anything. Because obviously I was gay. You know – I wasn't attracted to women! And I found when I did meet someone that I liked, I never really gave it a go, because I knew that I'd have to choose him ... instead of my *parents*. And then, I thought, I might as well give this *marriage* thing a go ... And so I agreed to go to Pakistan and be introduced to a few potential brides, and I'm kind of thinking that there's no fucking chance but ... just going with an open *mind,* because I felt like it was the right thing to do. And then I met this lovely lady, and I thought, *I don't know* – there was just something about her – I guess I went with a gut feeling – it was very confusing – coz obviously you don't want to marry this poor girl, and bring her back here and fuck up her whole life. And I didn't even know if I was gonna get it up. *(Laughs.)* On the night. And they come and check the sheets in the morning, to make sure that there's blood on the sheets. That your marriage is consummated.

M and R are grossed out.

So anyway, I called my friends, and I thought I was going a bit *mental*, I was thinking I don't know what the hell I'm doing, but I'm having a strong feeling that I – *this* is something that I should pursue. I stayed there for about nine months. I fell in *love* with a boy on my parents' farm. Who didn't speak any English, was completely different to me. Who I was seriously thinking of running away with. *(R goes to hug PJ – PJ breaks away, M and R hug gently.)* My head was like *really* done in! Coz I'd never been in love before, and I'd never had strong feelings about a man. And so it seemed a bit strange that at the time of my life I should be opening my mind to moving on from men, maybe that I've actually gone and fallen really hard for someone! And that was a very, very difficult choice. It was very Brokeback Mountain! And I didn't have many options coz if I came back to England I couldn't get him over here. And if I stayed there, I would have to let him support me, because I can't read or write in Punjabi or Urdu. And I would have to walk away from everything that I loved. *(R takes PJ to sit with him and M.)* And he totally understood that coz one day he had to get married too. A year later I married her. We've been married seven years and we kind of struggled the first couple of years, but it was great…

The first night I wasn't really sure what to *do*. I'd read an article in Vice magazine about how to do cunnilingus really well? So I thought, I'll have a go at that then … And it ended up that she's a – she likes sex a lot! So we ended up, having quite a lot of sex. Which was really really good, and fun. And then – I don't know whether the novelty wore off but … after a couple of years … we had a – we got – we had a *son*. Who's now five.

M gives PJ a line. M kisses PJ. R kisses PJ. Settle.

J: *(B – jealous, makes to go to J's bedroom. J – apologising.)* I prefer that people don't go in my bedroom. I don't really know what they're doing in there, I don't really want my lovely white sheets soiled by someone else!

B: We don't let anyone play in our bedroom either, our bed is *our* bed.

PJ: We had a period during the pregnancy where I started to do stuff behind her back … with guys at chillouts … because I found that I wasn't really attracted to her while she was pregnant? Which a lot of men aren't.

We went to a swingers club and … she found out that basically I was … into guys. She saw some messages from this guy that we'd been swinging with. And then we had lots of counselling and … worked through it, amazingly … and remember promising myself that I'm never gonna tell her that I'm gay, that's the one thing I would never, could never do because I have chosen now dedicate my life to this person. She's from like a very small village in the north of Pakistan, where she's lived quite a sheltered life? But then – I guess you know, things happen? And she can tolerate quite a lot. And we've still had like – lots of threesomes and she's not been … ickey about male on male sex, which some women are? I think? The middle ground is we're both allowed to do stuff with other people? Erm … I'm not really meant to kinda do stuff on my own? But that's the part I'm struggling with … I'm a bit of a greedy bastard.

PJ makes out with R.

B: *(To distract R.)* What are our rules for a sex-party?

39

R: There's no Bible, but you know, there's etiquettes everywhere – like, if you go into a dark room, don't get a torch out and start shining it round! That's not the point, a dark room's about anonymous sex! Try not to suck cocks in a dark room – you don't know what's on'em. *(Laughs.)* They might of just fucked someone and have shit all over their cocks!

J: I suppose one should always turn up … actually that's not even a rule … I was going to say should turn up clean! But half the people turn up here from another chill out! And, so, I'm like … 'Do you wanna have a shower? Before we do anything? Before I touch you for example?!' *(Gently aimed at B.)* Coz it's a bit minging, isn't it – when someone's been having sex with various other people for like … a day! And they just rock up at your place, and then start lounging naked all over your furniture!

B grinds on the sofa – laughter.

R: If you go to someone's house, don't invite other people over without speaking to the host or the other guys that are there! Because that's rude! When you suddenly get more guys turning up, your like, 'Hold on, who are these people? I don't remember inviting these!'

That's what happened this weekend! Before we knew it, we had a house full of guys who we didn't know who the fuck they were! We chose the ones that we liked *(Beckoning M and J to get PJ up.)* and then we said to the others – finish up – and the guys that we liked – stayed! *(They go for PJ – maybe R goes in for a blow-job.)*

B: *(Attacking PJ because of R showing him interest.)* I had a conversation the other day where the host was like – 'Don't invite him, he's Asian – people don't like that.' But I think because it's about sex, its acceptable. Sexual preference is not a racist thing ...

Everyone is stunned. It breaks the mood. PJ withdraws to recalibrate.

M: I hear such ... awful things like, the most horrible racist comments ... that just leave me ... like, so angry! Grindr profiles that say – no Asians. Can you imagine being some poor Asian guy like on Grindr seeing that? Profile after profile? It's horrible. People are just so free and open about what they want, what they don't want, they don't actually think about somebody else's feelings ...

Building to a fight.

B: Just because you don't like fucking a person of a certain race, or I'm not as sexually attracted to them, doesn't mean I'm not friends with them.

M: I can't go in that room, there's a black man in there ... But I'm not racist ... Really? ... People say these things, and I'm just like – you're a fucking cunt, like really, you're just a fucking cunt. *(They start to fight and are held back.)*

R: *(Trying to justify B without approving of what he did.)* I think this whole racist thing on Grindr is too hyped up. It's a preference. It's like being top or bottom. If you're a bottom, you want a top. You say to the other bottom – 'sorry love, it's not going to happen!'

PJ: I come across this all the time. People can be so closed minded. They don't know what they're saying – lots of people that contact me have profiles saying no Asians. Maybe my six-pack helps! They're like, you're different – I'm like – Yeh! There are lots of different Asians. You can't say the entire

Asian, or the entire black community doesn't appeal to you. That's just racist.

M is playing on his phone – probably looking to take PJ to a different chillout, B's next speech is attacking him.

B: We have a rule in our house, it's put your phone away – you've come to play with us – you haven't come to sit and chat to people on Grindr. *(PJ gets phone out pointedly and joins M – J and R are trying to calm him down.)* If you're bored with playing with us then leave. Don't kind of plan the *next* one while you're still with us. Yeh? But that's kind of our etiquette. Sometimes we've actually taken phones away and put them in a drawer! *(Laugh.)* Sometimes it doesn't go down very well.

R: *(Distracting B.)* Oh! Don't use up everyone else's Viagra! *(Laughs.)* I had … a box of herbal Viagra … Got – it got used up by everybody *(Laughing.)*

B: The problem I find with those is when you want them to work … they don't

R: They don't.

B: They always work the day after! Delayed reaction for me – the next day you're in work *(Laughs.)* sat at your desk with a stonking hard on!

Through the following J gives M and PJ the Tina pipe, which they take, and then forget about leaving. Then B and R take it. Everyone is medicated/placated.

J: People are very demanding about things like condoms and stuff. You know, if you want to use condoms, I don't see why I should provide them – there about, what? Eight, nine pound for a packet of three? Have a little … thought! That lube and condoms cost money! Especially over three days – imagine how many condoms you could go through! Hundreds! And those people that just fucking use them as fucking cock rings … you know what I mean?

M: *(Sheepishly.)* People do that?

J: Yeh. People will turn up. Open one up, tie it round their cock. They're just like, putting three pound, just around the cock! They didn't pay for, did they? I suppose I normally get them down the clinic! Stock up, don't you? You know when you go to the clinic and they give you one of them little paper bags, paper bags with about three condoms in it and a packet of lube? I'm like – they won't last me the tube ride home, love! When the nurse goes out the room I go raiding? *(Laughs.)* And I fill my bag full of condoms! Do you not do that? *(Laughs.)* Well you should do!

M: They'd give you more if you asked them …

J: Yeh, but I don't think they'd really appreciate that through me they're providing the half of South West London?

M: Surely they'd prefer that?

J: You say that, but STIs is their job – and without STIs, they wouldn't have a job!

Group laughter – it's all OK again.

B: We prefer everyone to just have bareback sex coz that's our preference –

R: it doesn't bother me

B: As a rule, if someone is for safe sex only – we won't invite them, because it makes it awkward.

R: We like top or versatile guys? 100% bottoms tend to be … submissive guys who just wanna lie on their backs with their feet in the air, getting fucked by everyone. That's not the play we like, so we don't play with 100% bottoms, and that's similar to the condom thing.

M: Does that mean you pick up a lot of STIs?

B&R: *(Laughing.)* Yes!

B: Yeh, you can pick up STIs … but that's the risk that you accept!

R: When you're playing bareback with someone that you've never met in your life, it's a choice. You think – I wanna go and have sex, but, I might walk out with something that I didn't have when I went in! You know what could happen, but you kind of step into that situation, *knowing* it could happen.

PJ: I did give my wife Gonorrhea once! *(He laughs – the guys don't approve.)* And I had the whole coward's thing of, you know, you've got to go and get tested, and grrr. And, you know, luckily I didn't have HIV.

M: I mean my ex was positive … so I know all about like detectable versus undetectable – I know what the risks are and I'm – you know – I'm more afraid of getting cancer than I am HIV. Coz – you know – it's maintainable now – it's not a death sentence. I know people with HIV for twenty years and, you know *(To J.)* they have bodies to die for, and they're gorgeous, and they look great – and it's, you know? There is still a stigma attached to it that people have, you know? Yes

– be safe, don't contract it – find a cure. But there are worse things to get in the world. Nowadays. Besides – I'm on Prep!

J: HIV negative people don't have any bother about fucking me, even though I've told them that I've got HIV. Whether it's undetectable or not … they'll say the risks are really minimal because I'm fucking you. It's not like I'm gonna cum in you … I trust you … God knows why! People go for it, don't they! I actually think there's lot of people that actually accept life, living with STI's. The time has come that people don't bother to go get treatment, because they know that in a week's time they're gonna have another one. *(Agreement.)*

R: So go on then, how did you get it?

J: I didn't get HIV from a chillout. I got it because I was a little bit naive when I was twenty-one. And, probably, didn't understand, necessarily – even though education is quite good – for our age group – that condoms are supposed to be worn! But then if you're with someone for three months and you both say that you've been to tests and all that stuff – to then – find out that the other person perhaps wasn't as faithful. Or not faithfulness, because you don't expect faithfulness, but you expect an element of – if you're going out with someone and having bare-back sex, don't go … don't go and have random sex in a car park. Then not tell the other person. Or if you do do that, use a fucking condom. And I know three months isn't very long. *(Starting to break.)* But if you've asked the questions that means that you're expecting the honesty. And so you make the decision to have unprotected sex. And at the age of twenty-one as I was, and he was like, twenty-three, we were both, I suppose, a bit naïve.

M: *(Hugs J – this story is to make him laugh.)* This guy, he was like forcing me, to date him … He was like please, please, be

45

my boyfriend. So I said OK, let's give this a go. I went away to Spain ... The day I arrived, I was chatting to him, and he was at chillout! And I was like ... Yeh! Great! You know that thing, about me and monogamy? Well you've just thrown that out the window. A couple of days later we're chatting, and I'm like 'Thanks for having the chillout – who said romance is dead?' he said 'How's this for romance?' and he sent me a screen shot of his Dean Street text message saying that he had Gonorrhea and Chlamydia. I was just like – fuck! Great!

PJ: My wife's six months pregnant. *(Group is stunned.)* Scary. But I think being a parent saved my life in many ways. *(Sort of an apology to J.)* You know, I used to risk my life a lot. With unprotected sex. And I think – it made me love myself more. Changed the focus. Made me less selfish.

R: I'm HIV positive too. I would not have bareback sex with a guy who said to me he was negative. If he turned round and said to me I'm negative, but I want to have sex bareback, I wouldn't believe him. He could've had a test, what twelve weeks ago? And then caught HIV within that time, you know what I mean? So! When we play we play with other HIV guys.

B: I'll play with negative guys!

R: Errrrr!

J: You do have a responsibility to make sure that everybody else is safe. But, ultimately, I always tell people *(M laughs.)* – well I don't always, I *generally* tell people – 95% of the time I will tell *somebody* that I've got HIV. Before I have any form of sex with them ... even though I'm undetectable, and the doctors say that it's, that it's virtually impossible for me to pass that on – and the risk is like 0.003 per cent chance of passing it on, right?

B: It doesn't bother me, as long as they're aware of my status, and they're accepting the risks. I'm on meds, I'm undetectable. And to be honest, in a sex party? No one ever cums anyway! Cum is like, *(Laughs.)* the rarest commodity! The drugs are the most evil substances on the planet, because they make you so fucking horny, you could fuck a Bourbon bottle! But you don't get hard and you can't cum! *(Group agreement.)*

R: And for two cum junkies *(Laughs.)* for two big cum whores, it's kind of argh!

B: Yeh! It is! Guys fuck and fuck and fuck for days when they're high on Tina, and don't cum. Can't cum.

R: The irony!

B: To pass on HIV, ideally, you have to cum in someone. And I cannot cum when I'm high! So yeh, I'll fuck with negative guys. Because I know the risk of me passing anything like HIV over … It's not gonna happen. And I don't pre-cum!

R: *(With regret.)* Neither do I …

B: I wish I could!

R: So do I … Because it tastes lush!

Group laughs.

R: I know it sounds really, really, really disgusting, but I like having sex with guys *(Through laughter – group are disgusted.)* that have Gonorrhea. Coz it's the best lube in the world …

B: Oh god, /honestly?

R: /It's kind of gloopy and *(Laughs.)* it just pours out of the end of your cock it's like its self–lubricating. I don't know where that fixation with me ever started … I think one time – I had sex with a guy who went, 'I'm really sorry I've got Gonorrhea', and I went 'Meh – I'll go to the clinic after, and they can clear it up!' And as he was having sex with me, I was like hmmm – actually that's better than if you were pouring lube in me by the gallon.

B: See I've had that many trips to the clinic, I'd rather just avoid picking up … things unnecessarily!

R: On and off between the two of us – the three of us, we've had STI's the last few months … but, we don't get them as much as we used to, because were a lot more kind of … not choosy, but more selective who we play with.

B: Yeh.

R: Than just fucking everybody, d'you know what I mean? If you go to somebody else's party, that's what can happen. You might turn up, there's no one else you like at all, but I'm so fucking horny I'll let a truck fuck me! I'm slightly more top? But drugs turn me into a big ass bottom boy! And I'll bounce around on anything in the room 'til my heart's content! *(Laughs.)* And then afterwards I get really annoyed, I'm like argh!!! I wanna fuck! I wanna put my cock in someone! Like, oh well, I'll just carry on bouncing around! It's the irony … For him … It's like Tina turns him into a big ass bottom boy!

B: But naturally I am a big ass bottom boy!

R: Yeh, but Tina makes you even more insatiable!

R: We went to a party in Manchester.

B: Ah, that sex party!

R: *(R thinks this story is funny – the others are unsure.)* This guy got more and more strange as the night went on. He was fixated with me. He *(B)* was upstairs, piss fucking or something – some guy – I was downstairs. The guy was sucking me off. And then he started rubbing – because I get off on people rubbing their heads? And their beards? On my balls ... but, when you've been, playing – for four hours, you're quite sensitive there anyway! *(Laughs.)* And he had the sharpest shaved head and beard that I've ever experienced in my life. And it got to a point where – even though I kept telling him to stop, he wouldn't. And I would try and move out of the way, and he'd keep hold of me. And he came downstairs from upstairs, coz he could hear me screaming!

B: I DP'd this kid with another top. And just after we came, we pissed in him, and drank it from his ass. We hadn't done that many drugs – so it wasn't, like, dehydrated piss – it was quite pure! It was hot!

M: That's the worst thing you've said all night!

R: *(He starts this story thinking its funny, then breaks by the end in real pain.)* My very very worst moment was when I was a full-time slave. I lived in with a guy, and his wife, and their kids. He took me to a sex club. He handcuffed me, both hands, both feet into a sling! Etiquette wise, you leave one hand or foot free – so you can refuse guys ... and – he then proceeded to ... He filled me up with vodka ... anally ... and obviously that made me quite lucid, and drunk and – to be honest, after about thirty, forty guys I lost count – I think I probably passed out as to how many guys fucked me. He came back about

– two hours later. He took me out of the sling and we went home! That was probably my worst moment. Which is why … I'm not as submissive as I used to be!

(R goes to B – Hug. B gives R a line.)

M: I met this guy at someone's, he drove me home, and I invited him in – we like talked and played and had a really nice time. He said to me you know, in the morning, 'I'd really like to see you again. Are you free tonight?' I could come and finish off the drugs, finish having sex, and then like watch a movie'! … I had a whole pile of … BAFTA screeners to go through, so I was like, 'OK, that sounds great'. He came that evening, you know, we're chatting, and we did a bit of drugs, he was looking at Grindr guys. 'What do you think of having this guy round?' I was like, 'I don't want nobody else here; just us, please', and he goes 'Oh, OK'. Half an hour later he goes 'That guy I showed you's at the door'. I was just like – 'What the fuck?' So the guy comes in … I let him in. He'd come all the way from Camden. And we start playing, I went to the bathroom, and … I overheard … Basically … they'd been chatting the night before. Neither of them could accommodate. So he arranged to meet him at mine! So they could have sex together. So he faked the whole, getting to know you, spend the night, watching a movie sort of thing, so that he could invite this other guy round to have sex. And, that just … I was just like, I couldn't believe somebody would do that. This guy started being a complete cunt to me in my own home. And I was just like 'Can you just both please leave! Go find somewhere else to fuck'. I kicked them out. They left. And it turns out that one of them, the guy that got invited around, ended up getting employed at my place of work.

PJ: Funny thing that happened to me, I was fucking somebody, and there was this playlist on YouTube or something. And all of a sudden Frozen's ' 'Let it Go' came on. And I came just as she sang 'Let it Go'. Everybody burst out laughing, it was hysterical. And I was like, oh god, oh god, okay! Traumatised now – I can never let my son watch Frozen again!

M: I was fucking a boy. And the boy kept on going 'harder, harder, harder!' I went harder. But the boy kept going 'harder, harder, harder.' I couldn't go any harder. I didn't know what else to do! So I slapped him in the face!

J: It is a really good way to meet people, and then possibly make friends. Most people might think *join the local gym*, or *try the badminton club* or something. But, you know? They just don't have the best Meph!

J is dosing and handing out 'GHB'. R takes it from J, thinks better of it and hands it to PJ who drinks it. PJ then takes his own G.

R: There are times when I've been at an event and I've been in a collector's mode. I've just gone round and got fucked by as many guys as possible to collect loads. And then walking home kind of like … Feeling it … Feeling it squirting out of ass cheeks as you're walking down the road is, is kind of exhilarating, That's the fun part!

B: *(They laugh.)* Yeh! I've, I've left the Hoist before now with an ass full of cum. And it's been leaking out whilst I've been walking home. … I've been collecting it and eating it as I've been walking down the street! It must look so wrong. But I'm a cum addict …

Movement Transition: R changes the music. Goddess by Chrome Spark. It moves to lust/sex. Just as M is about to fuck PJ, he G's out. They turn the music off – and lighting snaps with it to a colder/bluer

*state. PJ's screams/ fit continues for a moment in the stark silence
as they hold him down. They put him in the recovery position, and
he spends the rest of the play unconscious in the space. The mood is
now darker/pensive/reflective. It's that moment when everyone has
realised they should have got their Uber home an hour ago and now
they are too fucked to leave.*

J: Put something chilled on.

B puts on a more chilled playlist.

M: *(Puts on a hoodie.)* I met a guy online … He came round …
Sort of chatted for, like an hour and … then we started doing
some drugs … It was just really really really intimate, really
intense sex. It was a lot of fun. He stayed over and then I said,
you're more than welcome to stay the weekend because, you
know, if you leave now, I'm still high and I might go meet
somebody else and not have a good time, so … stay? Till like
Sunday. It was, it was really, really, really nice, it was really
really really intimate. We met up one more time after that, and
then … I cancelled the following time and then … he never
wanted to see me again … I cancelled because I *(Long pause.)*
he wanted to have a sober date. And I was like, terrified! Of
having sex with him … In sobriety … and like, not being able
to perform, or it not being as good – I talked myself out of
it? And I regret that – shouldn't of done that. Coz he actually
could've been somebody to have … have dated. But I actually
think good on him not wanting to see me again … coz that's
the same thing I would do. Good that he has his morals and it
sucks that I didn't have mine at the time.

B: I was at this epic sex party, a three day party in Berlin. I was
invited by a guy that accidentally dropped his lit cigarette in
between my butt cheeks in the smoking area! I was wearing
ass-less rubber shorts. He was so mortified, he invited me to

this party. It was amazing! He had three slings in his flat. A great big fuck bed in the living room. I brought my drugs, as you do, etiquette – put them on the table, and he was like 'Oh, isn't that so sweet'. Turns out he was Berlin's main Tina dealer! He had enough to knock out the whole of Berlin *(Laughs.)* He had this single-point sling … that you could spin around! At one point I had ten guys stood around me in a circle, all with hard-ons, fucking me, then spinning me a bit, then fucking me, then spinning me a bit, then fucking me! And they were fucking my throat at the same time. So I was just getting spit roasted, in a circle. For about an hour. And it was … the most … *exhilarating* … To be used continuously. I got fucked by all of them. I was HIV-negative at the time. Hadn't discussed … My status with any of them. But I was Hep-C positive. I'd only just found out. I was really shitting myself about it … Two days in, a couple of guys I'd played with before the party, who I *had* discussed my Hep-C status with turned up. And obviously tell the host. So then there is this epic debate going on between all of them in German. I'm like … 'Oh my god', *(Laughs.)* 'What the fuck?' But then, *they* were saying, 'But he's HIV negative and you've all come in him' They're like 'Fuck! What do we do?' We're in this really big dilemma. In the end, they went *(Pause.)* 'Just carry on. There's nothing we can do now. We've all been fucking him.' And he obviously doesn't really care. Just carry on! I've thought I was going to get the shit kicked out of me, because I didn't disclose my status. But at the same time, they were all shitting themselves because they've not disclose their HIV status to me! *(Laughs.)*

(Pause.)

J: Couldn't you have got PEP?

B: To be honest ... That point in my life, I really wasn't that fussed whether I got HIV or not. *(Breaking.)* Wasn't really something that bothered me. So, yeh ... Not good.

R: There's loads of times I felt unsafe. Sometimes we've gone to parties and I felt so uncomfortable that I said to him, 'I want to go – put your clothes on'.

M: I actually ended up rescuing some poor kid I knew, who was being forced to slam in a crack-den in Kennington by a very notorious person who, likes to slam young guys and then fuck them bareback, giving them HIV. Because he thinks everyone should have it, because HIV people are superior.

J: The problem is with things like Crystal Meth, the longer you take it, and the more you take ... You start to get paranoid.

B: So if you're in a situation with someone you just met, who has also been up for several days, and is also behaving erratically and strange.

R: And is also/ paranoid –

B: And is also paranoid, it's a recipe for disaster!

J: I'd been at the sauna. As I was leaving, there was a really really fit-cute guy going in. As we passed, we both sort of linked eyes and thought, "MMM he's fit". And then, during the chill-out someone invited this guy over? So that was really quite nice! In a fake, over-romanticising lots of drugs kind of way. But we really got along! The discussion came up about who is positive and negative, I'm quite happy to say that I'm positive, it's my house, and if they don't like it they can fuck off! And he was like 'Yeh, I'm positive too!' and I was like 'Aww, high five!' *(Laughs.)*

Eventually everybody left, but he stayed because, we wanted to have a nice night together just us.

But then it all got really, really … weird. Because he got really, really paranoid. I was like 'Right, come on, let's just get to bed!' We went to bed, but I couldn't sleep because *he'd* started making *me* paranoid. I went to the bathroom.

When I walked back in he'd got fully dressed, and threatened me that he was gonna call the police … because he felt there was someone in the *cupboard*. And I said 'Look, there's no one in the fucking cupboard – I'll open the fucking cupboard door, so you can see!'

And I was thinking – *shit* – maybe he's put someone in there! Fucking head-fuck! I'm just going to prove it to you, and that will be the end of it! But as I did, he came up behind me and put the point of the knife to my back?

Obviously in that situation, you're just like *'Fuck!'* So I was like – 'What the fuck are you doing?' He backed off, started dialling *a* number *(With scepticism.)* – the police? He said 'I'm in someone's house, and he's drugged me and raped me. I need help'. *(With sarcasm.)* Which obviously was quite concerning! He was holding the phone up so I couldn't see the number. I said 'Alright if that is the police, perhaps they'd be interested to know that you're the one with a fucking knife in your hand, and I'm the one whose fucking standing here, *naked, shitting himself.* Because a *psycho* just tried to put a knife through my back – so can they just get a fucking move on. *If* that *is* the police.'

I came in here. Then I decided to call the police. And he heard me do that and fled.

B: Did the police come?

J: Yeh! You've never seen someone move so quickly!! I ran around the place wiping – flushing all the left-over drugs. And then when the policeman finally came, I was standing in tracksuit bottoms, no top on, shaking. I didn't even trust that he was a policeman. I was like – I don't know whether to let you in. Show me your identification!' And he said 'I'll show you my identification if you open the door!' *(Laughs.)* I opened it. I don't know what the fuck … You do *seem* to resemble, what I would *expect* a policeman to look like. He must have realised that I was off my face. He was like 'Has the guy gone?' I was like 'Yes. Can you make sure that he's not around the area! And before you go, can you go in the bedroom and make sure he's not in the cupboard?' That was how fucking … the state I was in. When the policeman left, he said 'You really do need to pay attention to who you let into your home'. I was like, 'Yeh!' *(Laughs.)* And then realised that, despite flushing all the drugs and everything, I'd left all the sex toys, all nicely arranged like ornaments on the sideboard! *(Laughs.)* Piles of dildos! *(Laughs.)*

The guy rang me the next day and said how sorry he was. *(Laughs.)* He came back round the following weekend!

B: Was that okay?

J: No! *(Laughs hard.)* When he arrived he would be lovely. Sweet. Affectionate – which was why I decided I'd give him a second chance! But on the third time …

ALL: You invited him over a third time?

J: Yeh! *(Laughs.)* I just wanted a boyfriend!! We were here having a *little* bit of a chill like this … he said I'm just nipping down the shops to get some fags – he'd just had a G before he went, which obviously you're not supposed to do *(Gestures to PJ.)* He said he'd be five minutes. *Three hours later*, he returned. With his cigarettes. I was like – where the fuck have you been? He lied and said that he had G'd out, so he went to a friend's, to try and get some drugs. It just didn't add up.

So I threw him out – he wouldn't leave! Sat on the doorstep … taking G. *(Laughs.)* Crying!

About a month later a guy said 'His name wasn't Leo? Italian looking lad?' 'Yeh!' He just popped in on a Sunday afternoon for about three hours, then left, and stole a bottle of G!' *(Laughs.)*

(Mood turns very sombre.) So clearly, he'd got bored of me – fucked off for a fuck. And then came back as though nothing had happened … It doesn't take long just to go 'I'm just being fucked'. I wouldn't have cared – it's not *prison!*

(B suggests a slam to J, through the following they both slam, then make out. R is very aware and jealous – wanting comfort from B. M would leave if he could, but he is too far gone.)

R: He doesn't do it any more – but sometimes he would disappear for a couple of days – we'd have an argument, he'd disappear. Because his coping mechanism is sex, he'd go off, fuck around, and then I'd be like 'Are you alive, are you dead, what's going on?' But then my coping mechanism, is to shut down. *(Pause.)* But you get on, and you deal with it – d'y'know what I mean? That's why I think our relationship is more open and honest than any relationship I've had in my entire life. Because we don't do anything without talking about it.

M: I think having a monogamous relationship in London is near impossible these days … that's my honest opinion. Before

Mephedrone and G and all these drugs came on-board ... relationships lasted! I still know relationships that have been like twenty-five years. They don't do the scene, they don't do the chems and stuff. I don't know a single relationship since meph has been introduced that has lasted beyond four years ... Gay relationship. I used to love movies. I never watch them any more ... I don't have the attention span. Well, it's coz of the drugs! *(He takes another line.)*

I guess, for me, I see it for what it is from a very – not negative standpoint, but I do see it for what it is. You know you get the guys that are twirling round in their shorts, dancing, having a good time, because they're hot and high, and all I see is... A lot of pain. A guy that's become a friend, who was hosting a chill-out. And, there are people fucking on his living room floor, and on the sofa, and a couple chatting in the kitchen, and somebody getting a blowjob near the fridge, and he's like sitting in a chair, just like – looking around. And I was like – 'I know exactly what you're doing' and he was like 'What, what' and I was like 'You just stepped out of yourself and you've looked at it through reality's eyes and seen it for what it is, and you're just thinking this is the most ridiculous thing you've seen in your life' – and he was like – 'Exactly! This is fucking ridiculous! I need to fucking get high coz I'm looking around the room going this is absolutely ridiculous!' *(R does another line – as he comes up, he is unaware that his nose is bleeding.)* And I was like 'It is! ... it is! You're going to be sitting on Sunday night, watching The X Factor with your feet up on the coffee table, and you'll have forgot to that somebody was fucking on your table there. It'll be your home again. It's just – it's ridiculous!' It is, ridiculous!

R: The more intimate side of a relationship, like hugging and cuddling. The most fun about our relationship is when the three of us are lying in bed, watching a DVD. That's better than having twenty guys come and fuck around!

M: Yeh?

R: That's so much more fun. It's lovely.

> *(B and J have sex on the floor next to unconscious PJ. R does a line. Smokes. Cries. He has not noticed the line of blood from his nose. Music swells. House-lights up – no curtain call. The party keeps going till the house is clear. The sense is that it will go on for days.)*

FIVE GUYS CHILLIN'

de Peter Darney

Adaptation et mise en scène de
Christophe Garro

OBERON BOOKS
LONDON

WWW.OBERONBOOKS.COM

The french language edition was first published in 2019
by Oberon Books Ltd
521 Caledonian Road, London N7 9RH
Tel: +44 (0) 20 7607 3637 / Fax: +44 (0) 20 7607 3629
e-mail: info@oberonbooks.com
www.oberonbooks.com

A catalogue record for this book is available from the British
Library.

Cover image by Daniele Pintore

Visit www.oberonbooks.com to read more about all our books and to
buy them. You will also find features, author interviews and news of any
author events, and you can sign up for e-newsletters so that you're always
first to hear about our new releases.

Note du traducteur : j'ai tenu avec l'accord de l'auteur, pour cette version française à placer l'action à Paris et non à Londres comme originellement. Des noms de lieux ont donc été modifiés pour coller à cette version (villes, bars) tout comme le personnage de Mehdi qui est à l'origine pakistanais, et par conséquent certaines de ses répliques ont été modifiées également.

J'ai également donné des noms aux personnages qui dans la version originale sont nommés J, M, R, B et PJ pour Mehdi.

La version française de *5 Guys Chillin'* a été crée à Paris au théâtre Clavel le 22 janvier 2019, et a été jouée jusqu'au 28 mars avant d'être reprise au même théâtre le 15 octobre 2019.

Mise en scène : Christophe Garro

Création musicale : Sporko

Création lumière : Zoé Rodriguez

Chargé de production : Mickael Temstedt

Distribution

Julien : Vincent Vilain

Mark : François Guliana Graffe

Raph : Charlie Dumortier

Benoit : Lionel Rousselot

Mehdi : Jonathan Louis

Un grand merci à : Daniele Pintore, Emilie Paillette, Aides et notamment Pascal Barbarin et Stéphane Vernhes, Dominique Salmon, Antoine Cheret et le Corevih Île-de-France sud, Sylvie Krykala et le laboratoire VIIV Healthcare, le Cox, Abraxas, IEM, le centre LGBTQ de Paris, Franck Desbordes, Alexandre Mahé, Arnaud Gayet, Serge Lefox et Full Mano.

Personnages

Julien : L'action se déroule dans son appartement. Julien est pote avec Mark mais n'a jamais rencontré les autres avant ce soir. Il est affable, drôle, tendre, sensible et plein d'esprit. Son rapport à la drogue a une véritable emprise sur sa vie et il organise souvent des plans qui durent sur plusieurs jours. Au début de sa trentaine il était styliste avant que son addiction l'empêche complètement de travailler.

Mark : Il est un grand et bel américain qui vit à Paris (*Londres dans la version originale*) depuis plusieurs années. Légèrement distant, il est assez cynique par rapport à la scène gay mais ne peut s'en éloigner. Il est pote avec Julien mais n'a jamais rencontré les autres avant ce soir. Il s'occupe de relations publiques dans le cinéma, il est capable de maintenir son travail et est relativement aisé.

Benoit : Partenaire de Raph, il rencontre les autres pour la première fois ce soir. Il a un style assez « Bear/Recon ». La quarantaine, tatoué, bien foutu. Très sûr de lui, Benoit a un côté rentre dedans et une touche d'agressivité. Il est plus branché SM et hard. Il est directeur de casting dans le porno.

Raph : Partenaire de Benoit, un peu plus jeune, adorable garçon. Dans la vraie vie il a un look alternatif. Ouvert et honnête il parle aisément et s'entend bien avec tout le monde. Il travaille dans un sex-shop. Son addiction à la drogue lui a fait perdre conscience plusieurs fois au boulot. Il risque maintenant de le perdre.

Mehdi (PJ) : Homme d'origine arabe, fin de la vingtaine/ début trentaine. *(Il est pakistanais dans la version originale)* Pas très habitué à ces soirées, il ne prend pas beaucoup de drogue. Il est marié, sa femme est enceinte de leur deuxième enfant. Il a un léger accent n'ayant été élevé à Paris que partiellement(*Londres*). Dans son quotidien il a une vie hétérosexuelle de classe moyenne assez banale. Ces soirées sont sa seule possibilité de vivre sa vraie sexualité le rendant très chaud quand il se lâche.

L'action se déroule dans le salon d'un appartement. Cela peut être où l'on veut, dans le style qu'on veut. Il peut y avoir un matelas au centre de la pièce. Il y a un ordinateur portable ou une télé et un système de son. Il y a des pochettes de DVD porno.

Tous les personnages ont échangé sur des applis téléphoniques en amont de la soirée et sont arrivés grâce à Scruff, Grindr etc...

En travaillant la pièce, les répétitions peuvent mettre le focus sur le sous texte et l'historique de cette soirée. Qui accepte quoi, ou pas en fonction de ce qui a été expliqué de la précédente soirée. A quelle hauteur les drogues ont impacté ? Qui a envie de qui ? Si on cherche, il y a toujours un déclencheur sur ce qu'a dit la dernière personne et que la suivante va utiliser afin d'embrayer la suite de la conversation. Le but essentiel est de trouver l'histoire de la soirée qu'on va créer, au travers des relations, cause et effet et sous texte.

Prologue : Tout ce qui est en dessous est mis en musique et chorégraphié.

Tandis que le public entre, Julien est en train de regarder la Nouvelle Star sur son Mac. Il regarde en même temps les messages sur son téléphone, agité. Après quelques hésitations il sort puis revient avec des drogues dont de la Mephedrone. Il coupe et trace deux lignes de poudre.

Il regarde Grindr sur son tel, envoie un message et attend la réponse.

Grindr bipe.

Mark arrive, enlève sa veste, s'installe et sniffe une ligne. Ils regardent la Nouvelle Star ensemble.

Mark donne le feu vert en enlevant la Nouvelle Star pour mettre du son, un air qu'il aime bien.

Grindr bipe.

Mark s'ennuie un peu. Julien lui montre des photos de Raph et Benoit sur son tel et lui dit qu'ils viennent d'arriver. Mark accepte à contre-coeur.

Raph et Benoit arrivent. Ils se saluent tous.

Julien sort. Raph monte le son.

Julien ramène du matos (par exemple : draps, serviettes, shorts, lubrifiant et poppers).

Après une pause, les 4 mecs s'accordent.

Ils organisent l'espace pour le plan. Peut-être en couvrant le canapé ou en posant une bâche au sol.

Ils se déshabillent et se mettent des accessoires (shorts, jockstraps, harnais etc…)

Une fois en tenue, Grindr bipe.

Ils se jettent sur le téléphone. Julien montre les photos de Mehdi au groupe, ils acceptent. Il arrive.

Ils l'accueillent, il est un peu gêné.

Julien offre une ligne à Mehdi qui décline sa proposition.

JULIEN *(Baisse le son et demande à Mehdi.)* : Ben alors, c'est ton premier plan chems ? Ta première touze ?

TOUS : Ohh, Hou !

RAPH *(Avant que MEHDI puisse répondre.)* : Je crois que le tout premier plan chems auquel je suis allé, Je crois qu'à l'époque on parlait pas de touze mais de plan à plusieurs, c'était quand j'avais seize ou dix-sept ans.

JULIEN : Oui on disait juste un plan à plusieurs, ça fait un peu ringue non ? Avec mon ex, on avait l'habitude d'en organiser, à Montpellier. *Envers* Mark : Même si certains pensent qu'en province on prend pas de chems... ce qui est faux !

MEHDI : Non, j'avais environ seize ans la première fois, et j'avais pas vraiment réalisé que c'était une touze. J'étais supposé rencontrer un mec et puis quand je suis arrivé il y avait d'autres personnes. J'étais plutôt curieux, et un peu excité, alors je me suis mis dans l'ambiance.

MARK *(Voulant se joindre.)* : Moi c'était avec un mec avec qui je sortais, il vivait avec un couple qui faisait des touzes Tous les samedis, et c'est comme ça que... j'ai été introduit. C'était un peu, genre... étonnant. A cause des drogues que tout le monde prend. C'était comme... Un dépucelage !!

RAPH : On est restés assis, genre un moment, puis on s'est jetés les uns sur les autres, on s'est sucés puis on s'est enculés à tour de rôle. et ouais, c'était *(Il se marre.)* bah, comme ça !

MEHDI : Moi c'était pas vraiment un plan chems dans le sens de ce que vous faites là, avec plein de drogues. Y'avait de la musique classique ! *(Envers BENOIT.)* Je me souviens juste de ce vieux mec allongé sur un canapé, dans un bel appart, il avait une queue énorme sur laquelle j'ai passé beaucoup de temps, *(Rires.)* en fait c'était juste une bonne petite touze de dimanche aprèm.

BENOIT : Ouais, j'ai mis pas mal de temps avant de commencer les touzes. Jusqu'à la trentaine j'étais dans des relations exclusives. Et puis je suis sorti d'une relation de huit ans, et me suis retrouvé avec… le besoin de découvrir ce qu'il pouvait y avoir d'autre, voir ce que je pouvais trouver. Je suis allé dans un sex-club à Bordeaux, j'ai rencontré un couple avec qui j'ai parlé bareback et ils m'ont dit, hey, on va à une soirée après ça, tu veux venir avec nous ? Et j'y suis allé.

RAPH : J'étais à une rave à Montpellier avec des potes hétéros et tout le monde parlait d'une touze, alors je me suis dit faut que j'essaie. C'était un plan mixte, bi, oui à l'époque je jouais avec des meufs aussi. *(JULIEN et MARK font les dégoûtés, ce qui rend MEHDI mal à l'aise.)* heu c'était… *(Il se marre.)* très différent du genre de plan qu'on fait maintenant… Ce que je préférais c'était genre qu'un mec jouisse dans une chatte, alors je léchais tout et puis …je le crachais dans la gueule de quelqu'un d'autre. *(Rires.)* Tout comme toi !

BENOIT : Je me souviens du retour en voiture. On était six dans une Ford fiesta, Tous à donf sous Kétamine, même le conducteur. Marrant. Quand je suis retourné à la soirée c'était tout relax et simple, si tu voulais t'amuser avec quelqu'un tu y allais, si tu voulais juste chiller, tu chillais. Je me souviens m'être dit c'est pile le genre de soirée que je veux. Le genre de délire qui me convient.

MEHDI : J'ai baisé avec quatre mecs. *(Les autres le taquinent.)*. Je crois pas que j'étais bien doué à l'époque. *(Rires.)* Je crois que j'étais juste un peu étourdi. J'étais pas sûr de moi. Je baisais pas parce que j'avais envie de baiser, parce qu'un mec me plaisait. Tout était refoulé. La frustration, le stress, tout ça avait besoin de sortir. C'était plus genre, jusqu'où je peux aller ? Pour essayer de comprendre ce qui n'allait pas dans ma tête, parce que j'étais paumé sur pas mal de choses.

Pause un peu gênée.

JULIEN *(Tentant de changer de sujet.)* en parlant de paumé, hier soir y'avais un mec assis juste là qui s'est injecté du Caverject dans la queue.

MARK : C'est quoi ça ?

JULIEN : Du Viagra en injection.

MARK : O my God ! Waou ! J'ai beaucoup de mal avec les aiguilles.

JULIEN : A cet endroit-là oui ! Il somatisait de pas arriver à bander. C'est un peu triste en fait. On dirait que… si t'arrives pas à bander dur… ben quoi ? On voudra pas de toi en touze ? *(Il va s'occuper de la queue de MEHDI.).*

MEHDI *(Sursaute.)* : Je suis algérien d'une famille très traditionnelle, tout ça sera jamais accepté, tu sais ? Il y a une part de moi qui… Je m'aimerai jamais totalement, ce qui m'amène à faire des choses que j'aime pas particulièrement. Je dis pas que j'aime pas tout ça, mais je suis prêt à tout essayer *(Rires, les autres s'immiscent pour lui redonner confiance.)* pour voir jusqu'où je peux aller. Et c'est cool jusque-là, parce que je peux aller loin, je suis pas mal fort comme mec. *(Réactions des autres ; imitation de coups de révolver, etc….)* Alors oui, j'ai frappé à la porte, j'étais nerveux mais super hyper excité.

BENOIT *(Va vers MEHDI.)* : Aller chez quelqu'un pour la première fois c'est toujours un peu bizarre, surtout quand il s'agit d'un plan cul.

MEHDI : Je me suis fait baiser par plusieurs mecs, et puis après, pour être honnête, je me suis senti un peu dégoûté, et je me souviens qu'à l'époque je me sentais toujours un peu honteux, dégoûté par ce que j'avais fait. Mais c'était aussi un peu ce qui me plaisait. Que ça reflète ce que je ressentais au fond de moi. Un peu dégoûté de moi-même, un peu honteux.

Pause. Tout le monde est un peu gêné après cette conclusion. BENOIT sauve la mise.

BENOIT : Je me suis presque fait fister la première fois ! Mais je l'ai pas fait parce que le mec avait des mains comme des pelles !

MARK : A ton premier plan chems ? T'abordes le sujet comment quand tu baises ?

BENOIT : Bah, le mec peut être en train de jouer avec ton cul. A un moment il peut te dire genre, t'es branché fist ? Ou ça peut juste venir tout seul quand le mec te travaille le trou. Le fist c'est particulier. Soit tu kiffes soit tu détestes. Les gens ont parfois du mal à comprendre, c'est foutre sa main dans le cul d'un mec ! Ouais, mais si j'suis actif quel est l'intérêt ? Quoi qu'il en soit, si t'es vraiment branché par ça, c'est quelque chose ! C'est ce qu'il y a de plus proche d'une expérience spirituelle. T'es tellement connecté avec l'autre, tellement en phase avec tout ce qui se passe en dedans et en dehors du mec, c'est au-delà de la baise. Le fist c'est bien plus… sensuel. Quand tu as autant de toi au fond de quelqu'un, le plus petit mouvement est amplifié… genre dix fois !

BENOIT passe le lubrifiant à MARK. Dans ce qui suit, MARK fait comprendre à BENOIT qu'il est prêt à le fister, au grand plaisir de celui-ci.

MARK : Je me suis trouvé dans des plans avec des mecs de quoi ? Vingt et un, vingt-deux ans, qui se prenaient deux queues à la fois, qui se faisaient fister. Le fist fucking ? Je pouvais même pas imaginer ça à leur âge. Et aujourd'hui, ces petits passifs de vingt et un ans sont de vrais pigs voulant toujours des queues plus grosses. Des grosses queues, des grosses queues ! Et se faire défoncer tout le weekend, et moi je… *(Il claque les fesses de BENOIT et se marre. Il l'a taquiné depuis un moment. Les autres sont chauds.).* Waou !! Tu sais quoi, non sérieusement, toi, faudra que tu mettes un bouchon quand tu seras vieux pour t'arrêter de chier ! Et oui, ça arrive…

BENOIT : *(MARK aide BENOIT à se relever. BENOIT lance une pique à MARK.)* Il y a une vraie différence entre le nord et le sud. Dans le sud, les gens se marrent, tu vas à une touze, et les gens font des blagues, ils sont cool, ici à Paris tout est clinique. Personne s'intéresse à qui tu es.

MARK prend BENOIT dans ses bras et s'excuse.

RAPH : Je me dis qu'à Paris, la drogue a pris le dessus sur le côté festif. Ca manque le côté festif à Paris, non ? Ici, tu vas pas à une touze tu vas à une soirée pour te droguer et éventuellement tu baises… Seulement voilà, tu te drogues et après t'es incapable de baiser. *(TOUS sont d'accord.).* Les mecs restent assis, vissés sur leurs téléphones à Grinder, Scruffer… Les mecs se mélangent pas pour baiser, et nous, on se retrouve parfois… à devoir faire l'attraction pour que les autres commencent enfin à baiser.

MARK : L'attraction ?

BENOIT : Bah, j'aime bien être celui qui met l'ambiance.

RAPH : Tout comme moi !

BENOIT : Si je me trouve dans une pièce où personne ne tente rien avec personne, foutez-moi au milieu et je ferai tout ce qu'il faut pour que Tous se mettent à baiser les uns avec les autres.

MARK *(À MEHDI qui est toujours habillé, pour qu'il se change.)* : Le plus dur c'est… quand tu débarques… dans ce genre d'ambiance. Et t'as juste envie de… T'es toujours habillé mec !!! *(RAPH prend MEHDI à part pour qu'il se change/ déshabille.)* Tu pourrais peut-être te mettre en short. Relax !... Un short c'est bien, c'est facile d'accès, c'est bien excitant. Tu vas pas à un plan pour rester en calbut ! marrant non ? Tu veux un short ? Tu veux un shot ? de G ? Tu veux une ligne de 3MMC ? Faudrait qu'on ait des serveuses qui passeraient avec des plateaux !

MEHDI s'est mis en short. Appréciation générale.

RAPH *(Va vers JULIEN.)* : Y'a toujours un organisateur qui te reçoit dans les plans. Et alors moi, *(Il flirte.)* je fais toujours un effort pour jouer avec l'hôte… Qu'il soit à mon goût ou pas ! Alors quand tu commences à baiser avec un mec, genre ça réveille tout le monde, ils réalisent bah oui en fait… *(Il drague MEHDI, joueur.)* on est là pour ça ! Pas juste pour rester assis et papoter, tu vois ce que j'veux dire ?

BENOIT, RAPH et JULIEN deviennent très chauds.

BENOIT : Une soirée cul pour moi c'est des mecs qui vont baiser, et ça devient une partouze très Caligul-esque !

RAPH : Sodome et Gomorrhe. Allez, on s'encule ! *(Ils réalisent que les autres ne sont pas encore prêts à baiser, qu'ils font flipper MEHDI et mettent mal à l'aise MARK.).*

BENOIT : En fait, un plan chems c'est avant tout un plan cool entre mecs, prendre de la drogue, peut être voir s'il y aurait pas un autre mec dans le coin, pas forcément baiser direct.

RAPH : C'est avant tout se relaxer.

BENOIT : Oui, se relaxer et profiter.

MARK : On échange, on voit quel est le mood. Parfois t'es juste là pour la baise mais t'as quand même besoin d'un moment pour t'adapter… ouais ok, c'est un bon endroit, je reste.

JULIEN : Mais un plan relax peut tourner en plan cul.

JULIEN ET RAPH : Oh oui !

RAPH : Ou un plan cul peut tourner en plan relax. Si tu joues pendant six ou sept heures, à un moment donné t'as besoin de faire un break, c'est là que le côté chill out commence.

JULIEN : De toute évidence, l'esprit d'une soirée peut changer non ? Si deux mecs ont envie de s'amuser dans un coin, personne va dire, oh on est juste là pour chiller, personne ne doit baiser !

MARK : Je me souviens même plus de la dernière fois que je suis sorti et que j'ai dragué un mec, genre dans un bar, tu vois ? Boire un coup, puis baiser sur place. Maintenant, c'est tellement plus direct par chat. Genre le mec te dit *(Sarcastique.)* « Salut ça va ? » *(Il rit.)* moi, ça m'énerve toujours, en général j'ai envie de répondre « Ca va te faire mal ! Et toi, t'es dilaté, tu mouilles ? » Et une fois sur deux dans ce cas ils répondent « Oh oui ! » Et moi beurk, mon Dieu ! C'est dégueu. Il y en a qui me répondent « Je veux que tu jutes ta plombe dans mon cul de pute » et moi je *(Il fait mine de vomir).* « Je crois que j'ai une lessive à étendre… »

JULIEN : Plombe dans le cul… Je dois avoir ça dans mon ordi.

BENOIT : Nous on laisse les mecs choisir que type de porno qu'ils veulent. Le porno ça peut être un peu « normatif ».

RAPH : Moi ça me fait pas grand-chose. Je trouve ça un peu trop aseptisé et chiant. Ca m'excite plus de voir deux mecs baiser en réel. Alors j'ai tendance à mettre des vidéos de nous baisant avec d'autres mecs, ça m'excite plus. Sinon, je suis à fond sur Tumblr en ce moment.

Ils vont TOUS voir sur l'ordinateur.

… Les mecs s'exhibent, baisent et postent ça sur Tumblr. J'aime ça, plus que… le reste.

BENOIT : C'est du réel, c'est pas scénarisé et du coup plus excitant à regarder parce que tu sais que les mecs qui s'envoient en l'air devant toi prennent vraiment leur pied.

RAPH : Moi je me pose devant l'écran et je me dis… « Bah… Ils ont complètement loupé leur angle de vue », ou alors « l'éclairage est pas du tout au bon endroit », ou «c'est même pas du vrai sperme ! » Ou alors tu vois que les mecs ne sont même pas attirés l'un par l'autre. Ils ont aucune expression sur leur visage et c'est évident qu'ils ont pris des trucs pour bander comme ça. Ceci dit, je suis hyper voyeur. Je me branle en regardant les autres plus souvent qu'en participant. Je me branle en le regardant se faire tringler.

BENOIT : C'est ça, pas besoin de mater du porno quand t'as Ben et Ludo ici, ou Tom et Jerry, là qui se défoncent les trous.

RAPH : Mmh. Là je m'assois et je me branle *(Il se marre.)*. Pendant que les autres s'enculent, tu t'enfiles un gode, c'est bon vas-y, prends-en un aussi, haha, assis-toi dessus, enfile-toi ça dans le trou, puis enfourne une queue avec, plie-le en deux et enfourne-le aussi !!!

BENOIT : Hey, c'est ça, du porno interactif, le top du top !

RAPH : Ouais ! Quand tu, tu mates un DVD tu peux pas d'un coup dire... « OOOh, ouais, laisse-moi te fourrer ma queue aussi. » alors que si t'es avec deux mecs que tu kiffes, t'es là, « Tu veux te prendre deux queues mec ? » alors tu t'approches du mec qui se fait enculer, tu lui fourres un doigt, ou ta main en entier, et tu branles la queue de l'autre mec dans le cul jusqu'à ce qu'il jouisse.

BENOIT leur montre des photos sur son tel, ils reculent TOUS, MARK change de sujet.

MARK : Ew my God !

RAPH : Au début, moi, ça m'arrivait pas souvent parce que j'étais tout le temps en couple *(Réaction de surprise de TOUS.)*. J'avais tendance à choisir des partenaires toujours plutôt softs. Et puis j'ai eu une looongue relation exclusive. Je crois que vers la fin, j'ai... On a ouvert notre relation. Alors on allait dans un bar, on choisissait qui on voulait, on le ramenait à la maison et on se défonçait par Tous les trous. On prenait jamais de drogue, parce que comme mon mec de l'époque, j'étais contre. J'avais été hyper accro à la came avant de le rencontrer donc j'étais super fier de ne plus en prendre. Puis on a cassé, et j'ai... j'ai... fini avec ce petit chou.

BENOIT *(Énervé.)* : Avec ce petit chou ! Merci.

RAPH : Non mais on se ressemble vraiment Tous les deux, sur plein de points. On est là l'un pour l'autre. J'ai jamais été un mec jaloux, mais là, mmh, je le suis un peu de temps à autre.

BENOIT *(Encore plus agacé.)* : Quoi ?

RAPH *(Essayant d'éloigner la gêne.)* : Pas jaloux que tu baises avec d'autres, juste jaloux de pas toujours faire partie du plan. Mais... Argh ! On se fait encore plus de plans aujourd'hui que j'en ai jamais fait dans toute ma vie. Parce qu'on aime ça Tous les deux. Le truc c'est, tiens comme le weekend dernier, on est allés dans un bar, puis au sauna, on a ramené un couple de mecs chez nous, on a joué, puis on a fait venir un autre couple, puis un autre. Puis je suis allé bosser, non ? Je suis allé bosser quelques heures...

BENOIT : M'abandonnant à la maison.

RAPH : Et oui, je t'ai laissé à la maison avec eux, je suis allé bosser, puis suis revenu, on a remis ça, puis je suis reparti bosser, puis revenu et on a remis ça encore. C'est comme ça qu'on fonctionne ! Pas tout le temps, bien sûr mais *(Il se marre.)* mais... c'est comme ça la plupart du temps !

MEHDI : Comme ça vous organisez des touzes. Et vous en faites ensemble et séparés ?

RAPH : Ouais ?

BENOIT : Ouais.

RAPH : Ouais. Au début on faisait des plans séparés, mais... la plupart du temps on les fait ensemble, non ? Euh... ouais.

BENOIT : Ouais.

RAPH : Ouais.

MARK : Y'a des mecs qui font ça tout le temps et qui s'éclatent. En général c'est des mecs hyper canon, super corps, bonne gueule, grosse teub. Partout où ils vont tout le monde veut se les taper. Mais si t'es pas comme ça, tu le fais mais... tu risques un refus, puis si t'es perché, ça peut être encore plus dur, et alors c'est le cercle infernal, tu prends plus de drogue pour compenser, et là, ça le fait plus du tout.

BENOIT : Ouais mais, si t'es bien dans ta peau... ça va attirer les autres. Du coup on t'invite à plus de plans, et il arrive un moment où tu dois dire non merci mais...

RAPH ET BENOIT *(Ensemble.)* : Encooore !

BENOIT : Un weekend sur deux je vais dans le sud pour voir mes enfants, ce qui me fait un break avec le cul... Et ça lui fait un break aussi, parce que sinon... On s'arrêterait jamais !

BENOIT ET RAPH : Ouais ! *(Ils se marrent.)*.

BENOIT : Quand on part en vacances j'aime bien aller quelque part où je sais qu'il va y avoir des bars à cul, des bordels, une bonne ambiance de teuf.

RAPH : Pas vraiment des vacances familiales, hein ?

BENOIT : Non, ou alors ce serait juste pour baiser des pères de famille !

RAPH : Ouais, le sexe peut vite prendre toute la place dans ta vie. Ca peut si tu laisses faire...Mais...

BENOIT : Le sexe prend toute la place, complètement. Mais on a notre troisième qui nous calme un peu. Quand il est là on fait moins de plans parce qu'il est beaucoup plus timide que nous ; Il est genre... On est genre... *(Ensemble.)* Ouais ! Il est genre *(Ensemble.)* « Pas ça ! »

MARK : Marche arrière... Un troisième ?

RAPH : Ouais, on est un trouple. On est un trio polymorphe.

BENOIT : Polyamoureux.

RAPH : Polyamoureux, oui.

BENOIT : Polymorphe ?! Pff !

RAPH : Ta gueule ! Oui on est trois. Moi, lui et... l'autre. Ce qui fait que quand on est trois on joue moins, peut-être qu'on en a pas besoin, comme on est plusieurs ça fait une mini-touze !

MARK : Vous dormez ensemble dans le même lit ?

RAPH : Ouais ! On a lit ENORME!! *(Rires.)* Ca le fait grave.
Ca le fait non ?

BENOIT : Ouais.

RAPH : Mais ça peut devenir stressant parfois.

MARK : Est-ce que votre relation est la base de ce trio ?

RAPH *(Ensemble.)* : Oui c'est...

BENOIT *(Ensemble.)* : Non, pas vraiment.

RAPH *(Se rétractant un peu gêné.)* : Non, notre relation est un
peu secondaire... à notre style de vie. En tant que tel *(Sic.)*
non ?

*La situation est un peu gênante, les autres comprennent que RAPH
et plus amoureux de BENOIT que BENOIT de RAPH.*

JULIEN : Quelles drogues vous prenez ?

RAPH : Ce que je préfère c'est la MDMA. Juste parce que ça
te donne l'impression de flotter, genre woooh je suis super
heureux ! *(JULIEN donne de la MDMA à RAPH. Ils sniffent.
MARK s'approche et se fait une ligne. JULIEN commence à
préparer les shots de G.)* Je suis pas, pas trop dans les drogues
qui te font tout oublier, plus dans celles qui te rendent
heureux. Comme quand j'étais jeune, je prenais surtout
des extas, Un peu de speed, de la coke, mais maintenant je
kiffe surtout la MDMA. J'ai pris de la Tina, de la 3MMC,
c'est ce qu'on prend le plus en fait non ? Pas de ce putain
de cristal ice, ça m'a rendu aveugle !! Le G ça marche pas
sur moi, ça a tendance à me rendre malade. En général,
dix à quinze minutes après soit je dégueule soit je me chie
dessus... *(Rire.)*. Alors j'essaie de m'en tenir éloigné. Mais
tu sais ce que c'est, comme tout le monde aime le « G »,

alors tu te dis « bon allez ok, j'en prends un peu », et après t'es là « Et merde pourquoi j'ai fait ça ! »

BENOIT : Pourquoi tu fais ça alors ?

MEHDI : C'est quoi le G ?

JULIEN : Le G c'est une drogue liquide, GHB. Pris en petites doses contrôlées, ça te file un bon coup de fouet. Ce qui est vraiment cool niveau cul je trouve. *(MEHDI, JULIEN et BENOIT avalent leur verre et grimacent.). A* Mark : Tu trouves ça comment toi ?

MARK : J'en ai jamais pris.

JULIEN *(Choqué.)* : Pourquoi ?

MARK : Parce que j'ai vu plusieurs mecs faire des trous noirs à cause du G, la dernière fois que j'étais là.

JULIEN : Vraiment ? Et j'en faisais partie ?

MARK : Ouais !

JULIEN : Et je suis toujours vivant non ?

MARK : Ouais !

JULIEN : Je suis pas en bonne santé ?

MARK : hmmm.

JULIEN : A peu près… *(Rires.).*

MARK : Et les trois autres ?

JULIEN : Bah ils sont toujours en vie. Je crois !

MARK : Tu les connais au moins ?

JULIEN : Non.

MARK : Alors comment tu peux savoir s'ils sont toujours en vie ?

JULIEN : Parce que quelqu'un l'aurait certainement mentionné dans le questionnaire de satisfaction.

Rire général. MEHDI est effrayé. Les autres le rassurent.

RAPH : Ca fait le contrepoids avec la 3MMC que j'ai l'habitude de sniffer. Je me slame que depuis quoi, trois, quatre ? Quatre mois ? Je voulais savoir pourquoi tout le monde est à donf là-dedans maintenant. Qu'est-ce qu'il y a de si kiffant ? J'me suis slamé à la Tina et j'étais genre… Ew ! C'est quoi ça ?? Puis j'ai slamé la 3M et là c'était méga excitant. Ca m'a rappelé l'effet du Speed. Et c'est ouh !! *(Il fait semblant de sucer.)* et ça te rend ahh ! *(Il fait semblant de se faire baiser.)* Hey ! Je suis super bien !! *(Il chante.)* Lalalala…

JULIEN : La 3M je trouve que ça détend bien. Un peu comme une bonne bouteille de vin en fait. Ca file juste un petit… quoi que ça perche bien. T'es moins conscient de ce qui se passe, non ? Sauf si t'en prends beaucoup, à force ça te rend un peu parano.

RAPH : Je suis toujours dans le contrôle avec les drogues. Je me suis laissé contrôler par elles dans le passé, alors je fais super gaffe à qui prend quoi et à quel moment. En général c'est quand je me barre que quelque chose arrive, je reviens et…

BENOIT se jette sur lui pour lui rouler une pelle et le faire taire. Un moment gênant pour les autres. MEHDI se rapproche de MARK et JULIEN. JULIEN sort la pipette à Tina pour sauver l'ambiance.

BENOIT : Fumer de la Tina ça file des aphtes. Alors que si tu la slame ça rentre tout en toi et tu perds rien.

JULIEN semble tenté. MARK secoue la tête. JULIEN passe son tour.

MARK : Ca perche trop, beaucoup trop.

BENOIT : Tu peux la sniffer.

RAPH : Mais ça... brûle.

BENOIT : C'est galère à sniffer. Quand je slame de la Tina, j'en injecte un quart à un demi gramme d'un coup, et ça me tient toute une journée.

RAPH : Mais parfois les autres mecs amènent de la came aussi et là, tu te trouves dans la situation de... « allez on se fait un autre slam, allez un autre slam ! »

BENOIT : Et le plan qui commence avec un ou deux slams...

RAPH : Fini à trente six !! Parce que évidemment, quand y a presque plus de came et que c'est toi qui invite, « allez, encore un petit peu pour notre hôte ! »

JULIEN : Tu te dis tout ça, ça va et ça vient. La preuve, étant donné que je suis très généreux avec ma came et que les temps sont durs... et j'ai rencontré un dealer qui, bah, il me fait payer en nature !

RAPH *(À JULIEN.)* : Sur mon bras là j'ai une boule, je sais pas d'où elle vient, probablement d'un slam *(Rires.)*. Alors je me slame moi-même et si je suis pas capable de le faire, c'est lui qui me le fait, c'est le seul en qui j'ai confiance. Pas mal de personnes tournent de l'œil en voyant un slam.

BENOIT : C'est grave la mode sur le net de se filmer en faisant un slam et de poster la vidéo.

RAPH : Si quelqu'un me dit « je te slame moi », je fais genre « Er, ouais, mais c'est moi qui le prépare et qui introduit l'aiguille. » Et tout ce qui lui reste à faire, c'est de de de de *(Rires.)* pousser le truc *(Ils éclatent TOUS les deux de rire.)* et pis c'est fait ! Mais sinon, je suis un sniffeur. J'aime sniffer de la drogue.

BENOIT : J'aime pas, non j'aime vraiment pas sniffer de la came.

MARK : S'injecter de la drogue en intraveineuse, ça fait limite addict genre Héroïne ou crack. C'est pas bandant. Tu vois les mecs après un slam, la plupart du temps ils sont trop en demande. C'est pas excitant.

JULIEN roule une pelle à MARK pour le calmer.

JULIEN : Comme j'ai plus de boulot, alors je vais me percher un soir ou autre, je vais probablement pas dormir, ou m'effondrer vers cinq heures du mat, me réveiller à onze en ayant loupé un entretien d'embauche ou quelque chose dans le genre. Il reste deux lignes sur la table, alors je me dis, « oh allez, histoire de vider l'assiette ». Et beh non, du coup un moment après tu te trouves à aller chercher un sachet pour en reprendre. C'est un cercle vicieux. Tu vois ce que je veux dire ? Mais me concernant je dirais, quoi que, c'est pas, je pense pas, une addiction. *(Les autres acquiescent.)* c'est juste parce qu'il en reste.

RAPH : Pourquoi est-ce nous les pédés on prend tant de drogue ?

MARK : Attends. Y'a plein de gens qui prennent beaucoup de drogue. Les banquiers, les magistrats, ça prend beaucoup de coke, et d'autres trucs. Je connais des professeurs, des médecins, qui sont de vrais héroïnomanes. Plein de gens en prennent. Je crois que pour nous le sexe est une sorte de passe-temps, plus que pour n'importe qui. C'est viscéral, et la drogue décuple le plaisir.

Transition : RAPH monte la musique. Un air sur lequel ils dansent. Montée en puissance.

Le temps passe...

Ils s'effondrent en appréciant d'être bien perchés. Peut-être qu'ils se dévêtent encore plus. BENOIT et JULIEN s'affalent sur le canapé, se roulent des pelles et jouent ensemble. JULIEN baisse la musique pour

les ramener dans la réalité. MARK et MEHDI restent seuls debout.
MEHDI dirige la suite envers lui-même et RAPH.

MEHDI : J'ai toujours été gay. A quatorze ans j'allais dans des clubs gays avec mes sœurs et leurs potes gays. Dans la culture musulmane t'as cette putain de pression de transmettre le nom et d'hériter des terres. Tu sais aussi que tu auras en charge tes parents, alors j'ai jamais vraiment pensé que je me marierais pas, mais en même temps ça correspondait à rien. Parce que manifestement j'étais gay, tu vois, j'étais pas attiré par les meufs ! Mais je me suis rendu compte que quand je rencontrais un mec qui me plaisait, je me donnais jamais le feu vert car au fond de moi je savais que je devrais choisir entre lui et mes parents. Alors j'ai fini par me dire : « Pourquoi pas donner une chance à cette histoire de mariage ? » Et j'ai accepté d'aller en Algérie rencontrer des épouses potentielles, en me disant que j'y arriverais jamais, mais j'y allais l'esprit ouvert parce que je sentais que c'était la chose à faire. Et puis j'ai rencontré cette charmante jeune fille et je me suis dit « chais pas » y'avait quelque chose en elle, je crois que j'ai eu un pressentiment, j'étais confus, parce que bien sûr, je voulais pas l'épouser, la ramener ici et bousiller sa vie, et je savais même pas si j'allais arriver à bander ! *(Rires.).* La nuit de noces ! Le matin, ils viennent vérifier les draps, pour être sûrs qu'ils sont bien tâchés de sang. Que le mariage a été consommé.

MARK et RAPH sont dégoûtés.

Donc j'ai appelé mes amis, je pensais être un peu taré, je me disais je sais pas ce que je suis en train de foutre mais j'avais le sentiment que je devais aller au bout. Je suis resté là-bas environ neuf mois. Je suis tombé amoureux d'un garçon à la ferme de ma famille. Il parlait pas du tout français, il était très différent de moi. J'ai sérieusement pensé m'enfuir avec lui.

RAPH prend MEHDI dans ses bras, MEHDI s'en défait. MARK et RAPH se prennent gentiment dans les bras l'un de l'autre.

Ma tête était prête à exploser. J'étais jamais tombé amoureux avant, j'avais jamais eu de sentiment fort pour un homme. C'était ouf, au moment où ma vie s'ouvrait vers quelque chose qui était supposé m'éloigner des hommes, je tombais raide dingue pour un mec. Le choix a été très, très dur. Très Brokeback Mountain ! J'avais pas trente-six possibilités, si je revenais ici en France, je pouvais pas le ramener avec moi et si je restais là-bas j'aurais dû vivre à ses crochets parce que je sais ni lire ni écrire l'arabe. Et j'aurais dû quitter tout ce à quoi je tenais.

RAPH amène MEHDI à s'assoir entre lui et MARK.

Il a compris, car il savait que lui aussi un jour il devrait se marier. Un an après j'ai épousé la fille. Ca fait sept ans, on a un peu galéré les deux premières années, mais c'était super…

La première nuit je savais pas trop quoi faire. J'avais lu un article dans un magazine expliquant comment bien faire un cunnilingus. Alors je me suis dit, ouais, je devrais essayer ça, et il s'est avéré qu'elle… elle aime le sexe grave ! Alors on a fini par beaucoup baiser. Ce qui était super bon et cool. Et alors, bah je sais pas si c'était la nouveauté, mais deux ans après on a eu, on a un fils. Qui a cinq ans.

MARK donne une ligne à MEHDI. MARK embrasse MEHDI. RAPH embrasse MEHDI. Ils s'installent.

JULIEN *(BENOIT jaloux fait mine d'aller vers la chambre de JULIEN qui s'excuse.)* : Je préfère que personne n'aille dans ma chambre. Je sais jamais trop ce qui s'y passe et je veux pas que mes beaux draps blancs soient salis par quelqu'un d'autre !

BENOIT : Nous non plus on laisse personne jouer dans notre chambre. Notre lit, c'est notre lit.

MEHDI : Y'a eu une période pendant la grossesse où j'ai commencé à faire des trucs dans son dos, avec des mecs dans des plans chems, sans doute que j'étais pas attiré par elle pendant la grossesse, comme pas mal de mecs non ?

On est allés en boite, et là elle a compris qu'en fait j'étais attiré par les mecs. Elle a vu des messages que m'avait envoyé un mec avec qui j'avais dansé. On a beaucoup parlé après ça… et on s'en est sortis, et je me souviens m'être promis de ne jamais dire à cette fille que je suis gay parce que j'avais décidé de faire ma vie avec elle. Elle vient d'un petit village où elle a été préservée, mais bon, on change, et elle s'est ouverte sur pas mal de trucs, on a fait pas mal de plans à trois, et elle est pas choquée de voir deux mecs baiser ensemble comme certaines meufs. Notre accord, c'est qu'on peut faire des trucs avec d'autres personnes. Mmhh, je suis pas sensé en faire seul de mon côté, mais c'est un peu un peu la liberté que je veux avoir, je suis un petit bâtard obsédé du cul !!

MEHDI roule une pelle à RAPH.

BENOIT *(Pour détourner l'attention de RAPH.)* : Quelles sont nos règles dans les plans cul ?

RAPH : Oh, on n'a pas genre, une constitution, mais bon, on a des règles sur tout. Genre, si tu vas dans une darkroom, n'allume jamais ton portable pour voir ce qu'il y a autour. Le but d'une darkroom c'est de baiser avec des inconnus ! Evite de sucer des queues dans une darkroom. On sait jamais *(Rires.)* Le mec que tu suces peut juste sortir d'un cul et avoir de la merde plein la queue !

JULIEN : Faudrait toujours, ça me semble évident, se faire un lavement avant de venir à un plan, non ? Seulement, la plupart du temps les mecs qui débarquent viennent déjà d'un autre plan, alors chaque fois je dis « tu veux prendre une douche ? Avant qu'on commence ? Que je te touche ? *(Visant gentiment BENOIT.).* Bah, ouais, c'est un peu dégueu non ? Quand quelqu'un a niqué avec plein de mecs genre toute une journée et débarque chez toi, et se vautre sur ton canapé complètement à oilpé !

BENOIT se renfrogne sur le canapé. Rires.

RAPH : Si tu vas chez quelqu'un, n'invite personne sans en avoir parlé à l'hôte ou aux autres mecs qui sont là. Parce que c'est pas correct. Quand d'un coup tu te retrouves avec plein de mecs, tu fais genre « Hey ho, c'est qui ces mecs ? Je me souviens pas leur avoir dit de venir ! » C'est ce qui est arrivé ce weekend ! Sans qu'on s'en rende compte, on s'est retrouvé la maison pleine de mecs sans savoir d'où ils venaient. *(Incitant MARK et JULIEN à lever MEHDI.)* alors on a dit aux autres « allez hop c'est fini. » Et on a gardé uniquement ceux qu'on voulait. *(Ils vont vers MEHDI. Peut-être RAPH commence à le sucer.)*

BENOIT *(Attaque MEHDI pour le détourner de RAPH.)* : L'autre jour, un mec qui nous avait invité me sort « Oh lui je lui propose pas de venir, il est noir, les mecs risquent de pas aimer. » Mais bon, je pense qu'en matière de baise c'est acceptable. Une préférence sexuelle on peut pas dire que c'est du racisme…

TOUS sont abasourdis. Ca casse l'ambiance. MEHDI s'éloigne pour faire le point.

MARK : On voit des trucs… tellement horribles… Les commentaires racistes, ça me fout les boules ! Les profils Grindr qui disent : « Pas d'asiat ». T'imagine le pauvre mec asiat qui voit ça sur Grindr ? Profil après profil ? C'est horrible. Les mecs sont tellement libres sur ce qu'ils veulent ou pas, qu'ils réfléchissent même pas à ce que les autres peuvent ressentir…

La tension monte.

BENOIT : C'est pas parce que t'as pas envie de baiser un mec d'une certaine origine, que tu peux pas être pote avec.

MARK : Oh, je peux pas aller dans cette pièce, y'a un black ! Mais j'suis pas raciste hein… Non, Vraiment ? Y'a des mecs qui disent ce genre de truc, et moi j'ai envie de leur dire… « T'es juste un connard ! Un putain de gros connard ! » *(Ils vont à la confrontation mais sont retenus.)*

RAPH *(Essayant de justifier BENOIT sans pour autant approuver ce qu'il vient de dire.).* Je crois qu'on en fait trop sur toute cette histoire de racisme sur Grindr. C'est une préférence, c'est comme être actif ou passif. Si t'es passif tu vas chercher un actif, alors tu diras à l'autre passif « Désolé Bébé, mais ça va pas le faire ! »

MEHDI : Moi ça m'arrive tout le temps, mais en sens inverse. Les gens ont tellement l'esprit étroit. Ils font pas gaffe à ce qu'ils disent. Plein de mecs me contactent avec des profils disant qu'ils veulent des rebeus. Ils veulent se faire niquer par des rebeus. Ca me fait l'effet de racisme à l'envers.

MARK est sur son téléphone. Probablement en train de trouver un autre plan où amener MEHDI. BENOIT s'en prend à lui.

BENOIT : On a une règle chez nous, c'est : Range ton téléphone !

T'es venu jouer avec nous, pas pour rester assis à chatter sur Grindr. *(MEHDI range son téléphone vivement et va vers MARK, JULIEN ET RAPH essaient de le calmer.)* Si t'en as marre de jouer avec nous alors casses-toi. Cherche pas un autre plan quand t'es encore avec nous. Non ? Mais bon, ce sont nos règles. Ca nous est arrivé de prendre les téléphones et de les mettre dans un tiroir *(Rires.)* ! Mais c'est pas toujours bien vu.

RAPH *(Distrayant BENOIT.)* : Et vole pas le Viagra des autres ! *(Rires.)* J'avais … une boite de Sidenafil, bah ils me l'ont vidée en cinq sec ! *(Rires.).*

BENOIT : Le problème je trouve, c'est que quand t'en as besoin, ça fait aucun effet !

RAPH : Non.

BENOIT : Ca fait toujours effet le lendemain ! La réaction est toujours décalée pour moi… Et le lendemain, tu bosses *(Rires.)* et t'as une queue dure comme un gourdin !

> *Sur ce qui suit, JULIEN donne la pipette de Tina à MARK et MEHDI, qui la gardent un peu trop longtemps. Puis BENOIT ET RAPH la prennent. Tout le monde est stone.*

JULIEN : Puis alors, tout le monde se jette sur les capotes et le gel. Bah si tu veux utiliser des présos j'vois pas pourquoi ce serait à moi de te fournir ! Ca coûte genre quoi ? Dix balles la boite ? Le lubrifiant et les capotes ça coûte du fric ! Surtout sur des plans qui durent trois jours ! Combien de présos tu utilises dans ce temps ? Une centaine ! Et ces connards qui les utilisent comme cockring… Tu vois ?

MARK *(Penaud.)* : Les gens font ça ?

JULIEN : Ouais ! Ils en ouvrent un et se l'attachent autour de leur queue. Trois euros de latex autour du zob, allez ! Sans rien payer. J'ai envie de leur dire « OH ? Prenez-en à St Louis ! Faites des réserves. » Tu sais, ils te refilent un petit sachet avec trois capotes et un sachet de gel, genre ? Hey, ça me fait même pas le trajet retour jusque chez moi ! Dès que l'infirmière a le dos tourné je fais un pillage. *(Rires.)* Je remplis mon sac de capotes. Pas toi ? Tu devrais !

MARK : Ils t'en donneraient plus si tu demandais.

JULIEN : Ouais, mais j'suis pas sûr qu'ils seraient ok que je fournisse la moitié de Paname en capotes !

MARK : Je pense que oui.

JULIEN : Tu dis ça, mais les IST c'est leur gagne-pain, et sans IST ils auraient plus de job !

Rire de groupe. Tout va bien à nouveau.

BENOIT : Nous on préfère que tout le monde soit bareback, mais bon, c'est notre choix.

RAPH : Moi ça me dérange pas.

BENOIT : En général, si un mec est uniquement safe on l'invite pas, ça crée un malaise sinon.

RAPH : On aime avoir soit des actifs soit des versa. Les cent pour cent passif c'est… juste des mecs qui se foutent sur le dos et qui veulent se faire enculer par tout le monde. Ca nous branche pas, on se fait pas des cent pour cent passifs, c'est comme pour les capotes.

MARK : Ce qui veut dire que vous chopez un tas de IST ?

BENOIT ET RAPH *(En riant.)*: Ouais !

BENOIT : Bah ouais tu peux choper des IST, mais le risque à accepter.

RAPH : Quand tu baise nokapote avec un mec que t'as jamais vu de ta vie, c'est un choix. Tu te dis, j'ai envie de m'éclater en niquant, mais je peux repartir avec quelque chose que j'avais pas en arrivant. Tu sais que ça peut arriver, et tu y vas en connaissance de cause.

MEHDI : J'ai refilé une blenno à ma femme une fois ! *(Il rit. Les mecs ne trouvent pas ça drôle.)* J'ai eu la méga honte, tu vois, tu dois aller faire un test, argh… Et ouf, j'avais pas chopé le virus.

MARK : Mon ex était séropo… Donc je sais ce que c'est, détectable ou indétectable. Je sais quels sont les risques, et tu vois, je crains plus d'avoir un cancer aujourd'hui que d'être séropo. Parce que, tu vois, c'est stabilisé aujourd'hui, tu risques plus d'en mourir. Je connais des mecs qui sont séropos depuis, dix, vingt ans, et tu sais, *(À MEHDI.)* ils ont des corps de rêve, ils sont beaux, ils ont une super allure, tu vois ? Les gens stigmatisent toujours le virus, sois safe, ne le chope pas, faut se protéger. Mais tu peux choper des choses bien plus graves aujourd'hui ! Quoi qu'il en soit, je suis sous Prep !

JULIEN : Les mecs séronegs n'ont pas de soucis à se faire s'ils me baisent, même s'ils savent que je suis séropo. Indétectable ou pas, on dit que le risque est minime si c'est toi qui baise. Tant que tu jutes pas dedans !... Alors on a confiance… Dieu sait pourquoi… Ca rassure, non ? En fait beaucoup de mecs aujourd'hui acceptent de vivre avec des IST. Au point qu'ils se disent à quoi bon se faire soigner d'ici une semaine on aura chopé autre chose ! *(Acquiescement.)*

RAPH : Dis-nous alors, tu l'as chopé comment ?

JULIEN : Pas en faisant des touzes. Mais parce que j'étais un peu naïf quand j'avais vingt et un ans. Et certainement, je réalisais pas, même si on était éduqués - notre génération - que les capotes, fallait les mettre ! Mais voilà, t'es avec un mec depuis trois mois, chacun a fait des tests, et puis, tu te rends compte que l'autre peut-être, n'a pas été aussi fidèle que ça. Tu t'attends peut-être pas forcément à de la fidélité, mais au moins à une part de confiance. Si tu sors avec quelqu'un et que tu baises bareback, bah, vas pas baiser avec des inconnus sur un parking. Sans rien dire à l'autre.

Ou si tu le fais, mets une capote bordel ! Je sais, trois mois
ça fait pas long… *(Démoralisé.)* Mais si t'en as discuté avec
l'autre, tu t'attends à un minimum d'honnêteté. Alors tu
décides de baiser Nokap. A vingt et un ans, j'étais, et lui
aussi à vingt-trois ans, on était Tous les deux, un peu naïfs.

MARK *(Prend JULIEN dans ses bras et dit la suite pour le faire
rire.)* : Y'a eu ce mec qui voulait absolument sortir avec
moi. Genre, s'il te plait, oh s'il te plait, sois mon boyfriend.
J'ai fini par accepter, ok, essayons. Je suis parti en voyage
en Espagne… Le jour de mon arrivée, je lui téléphone,
il était en plan ! « Ok mec, super… Tu vois, toute cette
obsession sur moi, de vouloir être en couple, tu viens juste
de tout foutre en l'air. » Deux jours après, on se reparle, je
lui dis "Merci d'avoir fait un plan, c'est très romantique. »
Il me répond, « tiens pour ton romantisme », et il
m'envoie un screenshot de son résultat d'analyses
indiquant qu'il avait une blenno et un chlamydia. Et là je
me suis dit « Putain, classe le mec ! »

MEHDI : Ma femme est enceinte de six mois. *(Etonnement
de TOUS.)* C'est flippant. Mais je pense qu'être père m'a
sauvé, en plein de sens. *(Sorte d'excuse envers JULIEN.)* Tu
vois, j'ai pris beaucoup de risques. En baisant bareback. Je
crois qu'avoir un enfant m'a permis de m'aimer plus, ça a
changé ma vision des choses, ça m'a rendu moins égoïste.

RAPH : Je suis séropo aussi. Je pourrais pas baiser bareback
avec un mec séroneg. S'il me disait je suis neg mais je
veux baiser nokap, je le croirais pas. Il pourrait avoir fait
un test genre trois mois avant, et avoir chopé le virus entre
temps, tu vois ? Donc nous, on joue qu'avec des mecs
séropos.

BENOIT : Moi ça me dérangerait pas de jouer avec des mecs
séronegs.

RAPH : beurk…

JULIEN : C'est ta responsabilité de faire gaffe aux autres. Mais en fin de compte, Je dis toujours aux mecs *(MARK rit.)* ok, pas toujours mais la plupart du temps, quatre-vingt-quinze pour cent du temps… que je suis séropo. Avant de baiser avec eux. Même si je suis indétectable et que mes médecins disent qu'il est quasiment impossible pour moi de refiler le virus. Le risque est de 0,003 pour cent, tu vois.

BENOIT : Je me prends pas la tête avec ça. A partir du moment où ils connaissent mon statut sérologique, et qu'ils acceptent les risques. Je suis suivi, je suis indétectable et franchement, dans une soirée où tu prends des prods, personne ne jouit jamais ! Le foutre c'est genre *(Rires.)* le produit le plus rare ! Les drogues c'est ce qu'il y a de plus maléfique au monde. Elles te mettent tellement en chaleur que tu pourrais baiser un tuyau d'aspirateur ! Mais t'arrives pas à bander, et tu peux pas jouir ! *(Acquiescement.)*

RAPH : Et pour deux accros au foutre, *(Rires.)* pour deux bonnes putes à jus c'est… argh !

BENOIT : Oui grave ! Les mecs baisent, baisent, baisent pendant des jours entiers quand ils sont perchés, et ils jutent pas. Ils peuvent pas juter.

RAPH : Quelle ironie !

BENOIT : Pour choper le virus, en général, faut jouir dans un cul, et moi je peux pas jouir quand je suis perché. Alors… ouais, je pourrais baiser avec des mecs séronegs. Je sais que le risque que je file le virus est impossible. Et en plus, je mouille pas.

RAPH *(Avec regret.)* : Moi non plus.

BENOIT : J'aimerais pouvoir.

RAPH : Moi aussi… C'est tellement bon !

Rire général.

RAPH : Je sais que ça va paraitre très, très, mais très dégueu mais j'adore *(En riant, les autres sont offusqués.)* baiser avec des mecs qui ont une blenno, parce que c'est le meilleur lubrifiant au monde !

BENOIT : Oh mon Dieu, non vraiment ?

RAPH : C'est genre visqueux, *(Rires.)* et ça jute du bout du gland comme une sorte de lubrifiant naturel. Je sais pas d'où cette fixette me vient. Je crois que ça vient d'une fois où je baisais avec un mec qui me dit « désolé mec, mais j'ai une blenno », alors je lui dis « bah, j'irai à l'hosto demain et ils me soigneront ça. » Et pendant qu'il me limait le cul je lui ai dit « mmh, en fait c'est encore mieux que si tu m'avais rempli le cul avec un litre de J-lube ! »

BENOIT : Mouais, je vais suffisamment à l'hosto comme ça. Je préfère pas choper des trucs que je peux éviter !

RAPH : A tour de rôle nous deux, enfin, nous trois, on a eu des IST le mois dernier… Mais on en chope moins qu'avant parce que, sans être sélectifs on fait quand même plus gaffe avec qui on joue.

BENOIT : Ouais.

RAPH : Plutôt que de baiser avec tout ce qui passe, vous voyez ? Tu peux te retrouver dans une touze chez un mec, puis pas de bol personne te plait, mais t'es tellement chaudasse que tu te ferais défoncer par un camion ! Je suis plutôt actif en général, mais les drogues me rendent chaud du boule et ultra passif. Alors je m'empale sur tout ce qui passe jusqu'à ce que j'en puisse plus ! *(Rires.)*. Et après ça, parfois je suis super véner. Genre argh ! J'ai envie de baiser, j'ai besoin de fourrer ma queue dans un trou. Mais bon, je continue à me faire défoncer le boule. C'est le comble ! Lui aussi, la Tina le transforme en grosse passive du cul.

BENOIT : Mais je suis une grosse passive du cul !

RAPH : Ouais, mais la Tina te rend encore plus chaudasse.

BENOIT : On est allé à un plan à Montpellier.

RAPH : Une touze !

BENOIT : Ah putain cette touze !

RAPH *(Qui pense que son histoire est drôle, les autres en étant moins certains.)* : Le mec est devenu de plus en plus strange au cours de la nuit. Il faisait une fixette sur moi. Lui *(Benoit.)* est monté faire un plan pisse avec un mec. J'étais en bas, le mec me suçait. Et alors il a commencé à se frotter, je deviens ouf quand les mecs se frottent la tête, la barbe, sur mes couilles… mais là, quand t'as joué depuis quatre heures, cette partie du corps commence à être un peu… sensible. *(Rires.)*. Et il avait le crâne et la barbe rasés de si près, j'avais jamais eu une telle sensation. A un moment j'en pouvais plus, j'avais beau lui dire d'arrêter, il continuait, j'essayais de me départir, mais il me maintenait, à tel point qu'il est descendu à force de m'entendre gueuler !

BENOIT : J'ai fait une double pénétration dans le cul de ce jeune mec avec un autre actif, une fois qu'on a joui, on lui a pissé dans le cul et on a bu la pisse qui ressortait de son trou. On avait pas pris tant de drogue que ça, donc c'était pas de la pisse déshydratée, c'était de la bonne pisse, bien chaude !

MARK : C'est la pire chose que tu aies racontée ce soir.

RAPH *(Il commence son histoire en pensant que c'est drôle mais fini déprimé.)* : Ma pire expérience c'est quand j'étais esclave à plein temps. Je vivais avec un mec, sa femme et leurs enfants. Un soir il m'a amené dans un sex club. Il m'a attaché les mains et les pieds à un sling. Un conseil, laissez toujours un pied ou une main libre pour pouvoir refuser des mecs. Et il a commencé, par me remplir de vodka… le cul, et manifestement ça m'a laissé lucide bien que bourré, mais bon, après trente ou quarante mecs j'ai perdu le compte… J'ai sûrement dû m'évanouir avec tant de mecs qui me baisaient ! Il est revenu genre deux heures après, m'a détaché et on est rentrés à la maison ! Je pense que c'était ma pire expérience. Aussi, je ne suis plus aussi soumis que je l'étais avant !

RAPH va faire un câlin à BENOIT. BENOIT lui file un rail.

MARK : J'ai rencontré un mec à une soirée, il m'a raccompagné et je l'ai invité à monter. On a parlé et joué… on a passé un vrai bon moment. Et le lendemain matin il me dit « tu sais, j'aimerais bien te revoir, t'es libre ce soir ? Je pourrais revenir et alors on pourrait reprendre un peu de drogue, continuer à baiser, peut-être même après, on se materait un film ». J'avais une pile de DVD à regarder pour les Césars alors je me suis dit « Ouais, ce serait cool. » Il est revenu le soir-même, on a papoté, on a pris un peu de came, il regardait les mecs sur Grindr et il me dit « Qu'est-ce que t'en penses si on faisait venir ce mec ? » Alors je lui dis «j'ai pas trop envie d'un autre mec, je préfère qu'on reste juste nous deux tu veux bien ? » Il me répond, « oh, ok. » Une heure après il me dit « le mec que je t'ai montré est à la porte ». Et moi « c'est quoi ce bordel ? » Le mec entre… je le laisse entrer, il avait traversé tout Paris. Et on commence à jouer. A un moment je vais à la salle de bains et je les entends parler. Ils avaient chatté la nuit précédente. Aucun des deux ne pouvait recevoir. Alors ils sont venus chez moi ! Pour pouvoir baiser ! Il a été faux-cul « oh j'ai envie de te connaître, passer une soirée, mater un film », tout ça juste pour pouvoir ramener un mec et le baiser. Et là ça… ça m'a… putain, j'en revenais pas que quelqu'un puisse faire un truc pareil. Je n'ai plus vu en lui qu'un gros connard, je leur ai dit « Partez, s'il vous plait. Trouvez-vous un autre endroit pour baiser. » Et je les ai foutus dehors. Ils se sont cassés. Et la meilleure c'est que l'un d'eux, celui qui nous avait rejoint, a été embauché à mon boulot !

MEHDI : Un truc drôle qui m'est arrivé. Je niquais un mec et il y avait cette playlist sur Youtube ou un truc dans le genre. Et tout à coup ça a passé « Let it go » de la Reine des neiges. Et j'ai juté juste au moment où elle chantait « Let it go ! Let it go ! » Tout le monde a éclaté de rire, c'était hystérique. Et j'étais… « Oh mon Dieu, mon Dieu, ok ! ». Ca m'a traumatisé. Je peux plus laisser mon fils regarder ce film !

MARK : Moi je baisais un mec et il me disait « éclate-moi, éclate-moi, vas-y éclate-moi » alors je l'ai enculé plus fort mais il continuait à me dire « vas-y éclate moi, éclate-moi » je pouvais pas le baiser plus fort, je savais plus quoi faire, alors je lui ai éclaté la gueule avec des baffes.

JULIEN prépare des verres de GHB qu'il passe aux autres. RAPH prend celui qu'il lui donne mais préfère ne pas en avaler et le passe à MEHDI qui le boit, puis MEHDI prend sa propre dose de G.

RAPH : Y'a des fois où je vais à une soirée et j'ai juste envie de me faire doser. Je veux juste me faire baiser par le plus de mecs possibles et me prendre un max de doses de jus. Puis en rentrant, genre… sentir le foutre couler le long de mes cuisses pendant que je marche dans la rue, c'est hyper excitant. J'adore !

BENOIT *(Ils rient.)* : Ouais ! Je, j'étais au Secteur avant de venir ici, j'suis ressorti le cul rempli de foutre, et ça dégoulinait pendant que je rentrais chez moi… j'en ai récupéré avec ma main pour le bouffer pendant que je marchais dans la rue ! Je dois avoir l'air taré, mais je suis accro au foutre…

Mouvement de transition : RAPH change la musique. Goddess par Chrome Spark. Ca devient plus chaud, plus sexe. Au moment où MARK va pour enculer MEHDI, celui-ci fait une overdose de G. Ils arrêtent la musique et allument des lumières donnant un éclairage plus bleuté/froid. Les cris et convulsions de MEHDI continuent un moment dans un silence de mort tandis qu'ils l'allongent. Ils le mettent en position de récupération et il reste ainsi, inconscient jusqu'à la fin de la pièce. L'ambiance est maintenant sombre, pensive. C'est le moment où chacun réalise qu'il aurait dû rentrer en Uber il y a une heure et que maintenant ils sont trop défoncés pour pouvoir le faire.

JULIEN : Mets-nous un son chill out, tu veux bien ?

BENOIT met une playlist plus relax.

MARK *(Enfile un sweat à capuche.)* : J'ai rencontré un mec sur une appli, il a débarqué, on a parlé pendant environ une heure… puis on a commencé à prendre des prods. C'était superméga, hyper tendre, et très chaud. Une super baise. Il est resté et je lui ai dit « t'es le bienvenu si tu veux rester pour le weekend parce que, tu vois, si tu pars maintenant, je suis toujours perché, et je risque d'aller chercher un autre mec, et pas m'amuser autant, alors… tu restes ? Jusqu'à dimanche. » C'était, c'était vraiment, vraiment, mais vraiment cool, hyper, hyper, hyper tendre. On s'est revus une fois après, et puis, la fois d'après j'ai annulé parce que je *(Longue pause.)* il voulait un plan sans chems. Et j'étais terrifié ! De baiser avec lui… sans chems… et genre, la peur de pas être à la hauteur, ou que ce soit pas aussi bon. Je m'en suis persuadé, et je le regrette. J'aurais pas dû agir comme ça. Parce que il aurait pu être le genre de mec avec qui… avoir une relation. Mais je comprends qu'il ait pas voulu me revoir, j'aurais fait pareil à sa place.

C'est bien qu'il ait une volonté, et ça fait chier que j'en ai pas eu à ce moment-là.

BENOIT : J'étais à un plan épique, une touze de trois jours à Berlin. J'étais invité par un mec qui par accident, a tombé sa cigarette allumée entre mes fesses dans le coin fumeur d'une backroom. Je portais un short en latex ouvert au cul. Il était si désolé qu'il m'a invité à cette soirée, c'était géant ! Il avait trois slings dans son appart, un grand lit pour la baise au milieu du salon. J'avais apporté mes prods, comme il se doit, je les ai posés sur la table et il a dit « Oh si c'est pas mignon ça ! » Il était en fait le plus gros dealer de Tina de Berlin ! Il en avait assez pour défoncer toute la ville ! *(Rires.)*. Il avait un sling accroché à un point central, qui tournait sur lui-même. A un moment j'avais dix mecs en cercle autour de moi, leurs queues bien raides, qui me niquaient à tour de rôle, puis ils me faisaient tourner un peu, puis un autre me niquait, puis ils me faisaient tourner encore puis un autre me niquait à son tour. Et ils me niquaient la gueule en même temps. J'étais complètement embroché au milieu du cercle ! Pendant près d'une heure. C'était… méga… excitant. D'être utilisé en continu comme ça. Ils m'ont Tous enculé. J'étais négatif à l'époque, on avait pas mentionné mon statut. Je venais d'apprendre que j'avais l'hépatite C. Ca me faisait bader. Au bout de deux jours, un couple de mecs avec qui j'ai joué avant cette soirée a débarqué et l'a dit à l'organisateur de la touze. Et d'un coup y'a eu un grand débat entre eux en allemand, je me suis dit « Oh putain, *(Rire.)* c'est quoi ce bordel ? » Et alors ils disaient « Mais il est négatif ! Et vous avez Tous juté dans son cul ! Putain, qu'est-ce qu'on fait ? » Gros dilemme. Et au bout d'un moment ils se sont dit *(Pause.)* « Bah, y'a qu'à continuer, on peut plus rien y faire, on l'a Tous baisé, et de toute façon, il a l'air de s'en foutre alors… y'a qu'à continuer ! » J'ai cru qu'ils allaient me foutre dehors pour leur avoir pas mentionné mon statut, mais ils badaient Tous parce qu'ils m'avaient pas dit non plus qu'ils étaient séropos ! *(Rires.).*

Pause.

JULIEN : T'aurais pu faire un TPE.

BENOIT : Pour être honnête, à ce moment-là de ma vie, je m'en foutais pas mal d'être séropo ou pas. *(Cassant.)* C'était pas vraiment un truc qui me dérangeait. Donc… ouais, pas top.

RAPH : Y'a eu plein de fois où je suis senti en danger. Parfois on va à des soirées où je me sens tellement mal, je lui dis « Je veux partir, remets tes fringues. »

MARK : Je me suis retrouvé à secourir un pauvre gamin qu'on slamait de force dans un véritable repaire de drogués à St Germain. Une personnalité très connue, qui aime slamer des jeunes mecs pour les baiser bareback et leur refiler le virus, parce qu'il dit que tout le monde devrait l'avoir, que les séropos sont des êtres supérieurs.

JULIEN : Le problème c'est que quand tu prends de la Meth, du cristal, plus t'en prends, à la longue, ça te rend parano.

BENOIT : Alors si tu te retrouves avec un mec que tu viens de rencontrer et qui est perché aussi depuis plusieurs jours et qui agit de manière imprévisible et étrange…

RAPH : Et qui est aussi parano…

BENOIT : Et qui lui aussi est parano, tu cours au désastre !

JULIEN : Une fois j'étais au sauna. Alors que je m'en allais, je croise un mec super mignon et bien foutu qui entrait. On s'est regardés en se croisant genre « mmh, t'es canon toi ! » Et le soir-même, un mec l'a ramené à un plan chems chez moi. C'était assez cool. Dans un espèce d'irréelle ambiance supra-romantique due au fait qu'on avait pris un max de prods. Mais on s'est super bien entendus ! La discussion est venue sur qui est séropo et qui est séroneg. Je suis toujours assez fier de dire que je suis séropo. Je suis chez moi, et ceux à qui ça plait pas, qu'ils aillent se faire foutre ! Et il a dit « Ouais, moi aussi je suis séropo ! » alors on s'est fait un high five. *(Rires.).*

Puis les autres sont partis et il est resté, on avait envie de passer la nuit ensemble, juste nous deux.

C'est alors que tout est devenu vraiment, mais vraiment bizarre. Il est devenu complètement parano. Alors j'ai dit « Ok, allons nous coucher ». On s'est couchés, mais j'arrivais pas à m'endormir, IL m'avait rendu parano MOI aussi. Je suis allé dans la salle de bains,

Et quand je suis revenu, il s'était habillé et m'a menacé d'appeler la police… Parce qu'il sentait qu'il y avait quelqu'un dans le placard. Alors je lui ai dit « regarde y'a personne dans ce putain de placard ! Je vais l'ouvrir, tu verras ! »

Et là je me suis dit, merde, et s'il a foutu quelqu'un dans le placard ? Putain ça me prend le chou ! Je vais te montrer, et ce sera fini. Mais alors que j'allais ouvrir, il est venu derrière moi et a pointé un couteau dans mon dos.

Dans ce genre de situation tu te dis putain ! J'étais là « Putain mais qu'est-ce que tu fais ? » Il s'est reculé et a commencé à composer un numéro. *(Sceptique.)* Les flics ? Il a dit « je suis chez quelqu'un qui m'a drogué et violé, j'ai besoin d'aide. » *(Sarcastique.)* Ce qui, vu son état, était nécessaire ! Il tenait le téléphone en l'air pour que je vois pas le numéro. Alors j'ai dit « Ok, si c'est la police, ils seront peut-être intéressés de savoir que c'est toi qui as un couteau dans la main, et que moi je suis là à poil à me chier dessus parce qu'un psychopathe vient juste d'essayer de me transpercer le dos avec un couteau. Alors est-ce qu'ils peuvent se bouger le cul, si c'est vraiment la police ? » Je suis revenu ici et j'ai décidé d'appeler les flics. Il m'a entendu le faire, et s'est volatilisé.

BENOIT : Et les flics sont venus ?

JULIEN : Oui. J'ai jamais vu quelqu'un bouger aussi vite que moi à ce moment-là ! Je courrais à travers l'appart, pour essuyer, jeter aux chiottes tout ce qui restait comme drogue. Et quand le policier est arrivé, j'étais debout en pantalon de jogging, torse nu, tremblant. J'étais même pas sûr qu'il soit un vrai flic. Je lui ai dit « je sais pas si je fais bien de vous faire entrer. Montrez-moi votre badge. » Il m'a répondu « Je pourrai vous le montrer si vous ouvrez la porte ! *(Rires.)* J'ai ouvert. « Je sais pas trop mais... vous avez bien l'air de ce à quoi je m'attends d'un policier. » Il a bien dû se rendre compte que j'étais décalqué. Il m'a dit « Le garçon est parti ? » Je lui ai dit « oui. Mais vous pouvez vous en assurer ? Et tant que vous y êtes, vous pouvez aller dans la chambre et vérifier qu'il n'est pas dans le placard ? » Voilà le putain d'état dans lequel j'étais ! Quand le flic est reparti, il m'a dit « vous devriez faire plus attention à qui vous laissez entrer chez vous. » J'ai répondu « ouais ! » *(Rires.)* Et là je me suis rendu compte que malgré avoir jeté tout ce qui restait comme prods, j'avais laissé les godes joliment posés sur le buffet ! *(Rires.)* Une montagne de godes ! *(Rires.)*

Le mec m'a appelé le lendemain pour me dire combien il était désolé. *(Rires.)* Il est revenu le weekend suivant !

BENOIT : Et ça s'est bien passé ?

JULIEN : Non ! *(Il éclate de rire.)* En arrivant il était adorable, doux, attentionné, c'est pourquoi j'ai décidé de lui donner une deuxième chance. Mais la troisième fois...

TOUS : Tu l'as invité une troisième fois ?

JULIEN : Ouais ! *(Il se marre.)* J'avais envie d'un petit copain !!
On était là comme ça, en train de chiller tranquille… Il
m'a dit je descends rapido acheter des clopes. Il venait de
prendre du G avant de sortir, ce que normalement t'es pas
censé faire *(Regard vers MEHDI.)*. Il a dit j'en ai pour cinq
minutes. Il est revenu trois heures après, avec ses clopes.
Je lui ai dit « Putain mais t'étais où ? » Il s'est allongé et
m'a dit qu'il avait fait un trou noir, alors il est allé chez
des potes pour essayer d'avoir d'autres drogues, ce qui n'a
aucun sens.

Alors je l'ai foutu dehors. Il voulait pas partir ! Il est resté
assis sur le pas de la porte, à prendre du G *(Rires.)*. A
chialer…

Environ un mois après un mec me dit « Il s'appelait pas
Leo ? Type italien, ouais, il s'est pointé un dimanche
aprèm, il est resté environ trois heures et s'est barré en
volant une bouteille de G ! » *(Rires.)*.

L'ambiance devient assez sombre.

Clairement, il en avait marre de moi. Tout foutre en l'air
pour un coup. C'est pas compliqué de dire « je viens juste
de me faire tirer. » Je lui en aurais pas voulu, je le gardais
pas en prison !

*BENOIT propose un slam à JULIEN. Dans ce qui suit, ils se slament et
baisent. RAPH est très conscient et jaloux. Il voudrait que BENOIT le
réconforte. MARK partirait s'il le pouvait mais il est bien trop barré.*

RAPH : Il le fait plus trop maintenant, mais parfois il
disparaissait pendant deux jours. On avait une engueulade
et il disparaissait. Parce que son échappatoire quand ça va
pas, c'est le sexe. Il va sortir et baiser à tout va. Et moi je
me demande où il est, s'il est mort ou vivant. A l'inverse,
moi j'éteins tout et je me renferme. *(Pause.)* Mais bon on
fait avec, et on avance. Tu vois ce que je veux dire ? C'est

pour ça que je me dis que notre relation est plus sincère et ouverte que n'importe quelle autre. Parce qu'on fait rien sans en parler.

MARK : Je crois qu'il est impossible d'avoir une relation monogame à Paris aujourd'hui… Franchement. Avant que la Mephedrone, le G, et toutes ces drogues débarquent, les mecs avaient des relations qui duraient. J'en connais qui sont encore ensemble après vingt-cinq ans ! Mais ils sont pas dans le milieu, ils sont pas dans les chems et tout ça. Je connais pas un couple, depuis que la Meph a débarqué, qui ait duré plus de quatre ans… entre gays. J'aimais aller au ciné, maintenant c'est fini, je suis plus capable de rester attentif. Et ouais, c'est la faute aux prods. *(Il reprend une ligne.)*

Je crois, de mon point de vue, je vois les choses, pas négativement, mais, je les vois pour ce qu'elles sont. Tu vois, les mecs tournent en short, dansent, s'amusent, ils sont chauds, ils sont perchés, et tout ce que je vois c'est… une grande douleur. J'étais à un plan chez un mec qui est devenu un pote, y'avait des mecs partout qui baisaient dans son salon, sur son canapé, un couple discutait dans la cuisine et un mec se faisait sucer à côté du frigo. Mon pote était assis sur une chaise, à regarder autour de lui. Je lui ai dit « Je sais exactement ce que tu penses. » et lui « quoi ? Quoi ? » « Tu viens de prendre du recul et tu regardes ce qui se passe ici avec un regard lucide, et tu vois la réalité. Et tu te dis que c'est la chose la plus ridicule que t'aies vue de toute ta vie. Et il m'a répondu « Exact. C'est complètement débile. Va falloir que je me perche, parce que sinon je regarde autour de moi et je me dis c'est carrément débile tout ça ! »

RAPH se reprend une ligne. En se relevant il ne fait pas attention à son nez qui saigne.

Et je lui ai dit « ouais, c'est vrai, et tu vas passer ta soirée de dimanche sur ton canap à comater devant la Nouvelle Star les pieds sur ta table basse, et t'auras oublié que quelqu'un s'est fait enculer sur cette même table. Tu seras chez toi à nouveau. C'est ridicule. Complètement ridicule ! »

RAPH : Le meilleur dans une relation, c'est les caresses et les étreintes. Ce qu'il y a de meilleur dans notre relation, c'est quand on est Tous les trois dans le lit et qu'on regarde un DVD. C'est mieux que d'avoir vingt mecs avec qui baiser.

MARK : Ah ouais ?

RAPH : C'est tellement plus cool. C'est beau.

BENOIT et JULIEN baisent sur le sol à côté de MEHDI qui est resté inconscient. RAPH reprend une ligne, fume, pleure. Il n'a pas fait attention au trait de sang qui coule de son nez. La musique est comme un tourbillon. La salle s'éclaire. Pas de fermé de rideau. Le plan continue jusqu'à ce que la salle soit complètement vidée, laissant supposer que tout ça peut durer encore pendant des jours...

FIN

'Raw and honest… for some gay men this will seem like a different world, but for a lot of gay men this kind of party will be achingly familiar.'
Gay Star News

'Darney has done an exceptional job weaving the stories together into the five distinct characters, creating a clever narrative… This is a show that catches you by surprise and forces you to consider really difficult questions.'
Broadway World.

'Relaying experiences and issues relating to homosexuality in BME cultures, a narrative often overlooked.'
Eqview

(Chill-outs) 'Can be scary, hilarious, ridiculous, sexy or all of the above. And Peter Darney's brave, sensory play captured all of that perfectly. The portrayal was flawlessly accurate, down to the last pair of nylon shorts. In a stark, realistic, totally un-preachy way, he painted a very real portrait of a situation more and more urban gay men are finding themselves facing.
5 Guys Chillin' reminded me of the faded glamour of a Stockwell flat at 7am on a Tuesday, without the glamour and more of an unabashed frankness.'
QX Magazine

'This is as confronting as theatre gets.'
British Theatre

'Extraordinarily powerful.'
British Theatre Guide.